OPPOSING
VIEWPOINTS®
SERIES

Health Care

Other Books of Related Interest

Opposing Viewpoints Series

Alternative Medicine

Government Spending

Medicine

Current Controversies Series

Health Care

Mental Health

Prescription Drugs

At Issue Series

Are Americans Overmedicated?

Cancer

Organ Transplants

"Congress shall make
no law . . . abridging
the freedom of speech,
or of the press."

First Amendment to the U.S. Constitution

The basic foundation of our democracy is the First Amendment guarantee of freedom of expression. The Opposing Viewpoints Series is dedicated to the concept of this basic freedom and the idea that it is more important to practice it than to enshrine it.

Health Care

David M. Haugen, Book Editor

GREENHAVEN PRESS
A part of Gale, Cengage Learning

GALE
CENGAGE Learning

Detroit • New York • San Francisco • New Haven, Conn • Waterville, Maine • London

GALE
CENGAGE Learning

Christine Nasso, *Publisher*
Elizabeth Des Chenes, *Managing Editor*

© 2008 Greenhaven Press, a part of Gale, Cengage Learning.

Gale and Greenhaven Press are registered trademarks used herein under license.

For more information, contact:
Greenhaven Press
27500 Drake Rd.
Farmington Hills, MI 48331-3535
Or you can visit our Internet site at gale.cengage.com

For product information and technology assistance, contact us at

Gale Customer Support, 1-800-877-4253
For permission to use material from this text or product, submit all requests online at www.cengage.com/permissions

Further permissions questions can be emailed to permissionrequest@cengage.com

Articles in Greenhaven Press anthologies are often edited for length to meet page requirements. In addition, original titles of these works are changed to clearly present the main thesis and to explicitly indicate the author's opinion. Every effort is made to ensure that Greenhaven Press accurately reflects the original intent of the authors. Every effort has been made to trace the owners of copyrighted material.

Cover photograph reproduced by permission of Martin Barraud/OJO Images/Getty Images.

LIBRARY OF CONGRESS CATALOGING-IN-PUBLICATION DATA

Health care / David M. Haugen, book editor.
    p. cm. -- (Opposing viewpoints)
    Includes bibliographical references and index.
    ISBN-13: 978-0-7377-4006-6 (hardcover)
    ISBN-13: 978-0-7377-4007-3 (pbk.)
    1. Health care reform--United States. 2. Medical policy--United States. I. Haugen, David M., 1969-
    RA395.A3H382 2008
    362.1'04250973--dc22

                                    2007050851

Printed in the United States of America
1 2 3 4 5 6 7 12 11 10 09 08

Contents

Chapter 4: How Should State Health Care Programs Be Altered?

Why Consider
Opposing Viewpoints?

> *"The only way in which a human being can make some approach to knowing the whole of a subject is by hearing what can be said about it by persons of every variety of opinion and studying all modes in which it can be looked at by every character of mind. No wise man ever acquired his wisdom in any mode but this."*
>
> John Stuart Mill

In our media-intensive culture it is not difficult to find differing opinions. Thousands of newspapers and magazines and dozens of radio and television talk shows resound with differing points of view. The difficulty lies in deciding which opinion to agree with and which "experts" seem the most credible. The more inundated we become with differing opinions and claims, the more essential it is to hone critical reading and thinking skills to evaluate these ideas. Opposing Viewpoints books address this problem directly by presenting stimulating debates that can be used to enhance and teach these skills. The varied opinions contained in each book examine many different aspects of a single issue. While examining these conveniently edited opposing views, readers can develop critical thinking skills such as the ability to compare and contrast authors' credibility, facts, argumentation styles, use of persuasive techniques, and other stylistic tools. In short, the Opposing Viewpoints Series is an ideal way to attain the higher-level thinking and reading skills so essential in a culture of diverse and contradictory opinions.

In addition to providing a tool for critical thinking, Opposing Viewpoints books challenge readers to question their own strongly held opinions and assumptions. Most people form their opinions on the basis of upbringing, peer pressure, and personal, cultural, or professional bias. By reading carefully balanced opposing views, readers must directly confront new ideas as well as the opinions of those with whom they disagree. This is not to simplistically argue that everyone who reads opposing views will—or should—change his or her opinion. Instead, the series enhances readers' understanding of their own views by encouraging confrontation with opposing ideas. Careful examination of others' views can lead to the readers' understanding of the logical inconsistencies in their own opinions, perspective on why they hold an opinion, and the consideration of the possibility that their opinion requires further evaluation.

Evaluating Other Opinions

To ensure that this type of examination occurs, Opposing Viewpoints books present all types of opinions. Prominent spokespeople on different sides of each issue as well as well-known professionals from many disciplines challenge the reader. An additional goal of the series is to provide a forum for other, less known, or even unpopular viewpoints. The opinion of an ordinary person who has had to make the decision to cut off life support from a terminally ill relative, for example, may be just as valuable and provide just as much insight as a medical ethicist's professional opinion. The editors have two additional purposes in including these less known views. One, the editors encourage readers to respect others' opinions—even when not enhanced by professional credibility. It is only by reading or listening to and objectively evaluating others' ideas that one can determine whether they are worthy of consideration. Two, the inclusion of such viewpoints encourages the important critical thinking skill of objectively evaluating an author's credentials and bias. This evaluation will illuminate an author's reasons for taking a particular stance on an issue and will aid in readers' evaluation of the author's ideas.

It is our hope that these books will give readers a deeper understanding of the issues debated and an appreciation of the complexity of even seemingly simple issues when good and honest people disagree. This awareness is particularly important in a democratic society such as ours in which people enter into public debate to determine the common good. Those with whom one disagrees should not be regarded as enemies but rather as people whose views deserve careful examination and may shed light on one's own.

Thomas Jefferson once said that "difference of opinion leads to inquiry, and inquiry to truth." Jefferson, a broadly educated man, argued that "if a nation expects to be ignorant and free . . . it expects what never was and never will be." As individuals and as a nation, it is imperative that we consider the opinions of others and examine them with skill and discernment. The Opposing Viewpoints Series is intended to help readers achieve this goal.

David L. Bender and Bruno Leone,
Founders

Introduction

> *The good news is that policymakers have a full toolbox for pursuing goals regarding health care costs and spending. They can use government resources and leadership to help improve health care. They can change federal programs to influence both access to care and federal spending. And they can use tax policy to support and shape the market for health insurance and health care.*
>
> *The bad news is that both problems and solutions are complicated. Does the United States spend too much on health care, or not? How should society allocate its resources among members? And how should policymakers set priorities among competing goals and interests? Even assuming agreement on these questions, the Congress faces difficult challenges in choosing the best combination of policy tools for achieving whatever objective is adopted.*
>
> Jennifer Jenson,
> Congressional Research Service Report,
> March 31, 2006

One of the most talked about issues in America for the last quarter of a century is the rising cost of health care. Since the 1980s, health care spending has increased nearly ten-fold and, in 2007, consumes around 16 percent of the gross domestic product (GDP) of the United States, or just over

2 trillion dollars. In comparison, the majority of other developed nations spend less than 8 percent of their GDP on health care. According to the Commonwealth Fund, a private foundation devoted to improving access to high-performance health care, more than 13 million American families paid out-of-pocket costs for health services that equaled or exceeded 10 percent of their household income. How to manage these costs has become the concern of presidents, politicians, health care organizations, insurance companies, editorialists, and consumers.

Until the mid-1980s, health care costs were not such a pressing national issue. Most health costs were covered by private insurers who contracted with employers to pay for the medical expenses of their employees. Employees paid a co-payment (that ranged from 10 to 20 percent), and the insurer was billed for the rest. This insurance was a fringe benefit of employment and served the employers well by providing them with a tax break for the insurance costs. However, as health care insurance premiums began to rise, many businesses found it too expensive to deal with private insurers who seemingly had no way of keeping their costs down. Employers began dropping private insurance to contract instead with managed care providers that sought to control costs by limiting care to a specific benefits package. The most popular type of managed care was—and remains—health maintenance organizations (HMOs), which require patients to use a predetermined network of physicians and hospitals that are continually reviewed for their performance and cost.

Those who favor managed care believe that HMOs and other providers stop doctors from ordering useless tests, prescribing expensive medicines when generic alternatives are available, and generally overspending. Managed care is also touted as encouraging patient responsibility to seek care early through a low physician-visit co-payment and therefore avoid the high medical costs of hospital stays and treatment for untended illness. Critics of this system contend that managed care forces patients to seek the cheapest care rather than the most helpful or best care. By compelling patients to see specific doctors, consumers often complain that they have to leave trusted physicians who are not part of an HMO network. Patients also cannot see a specialist without a referral from a network doctor, leaving patients feeling as if they have little say in choosing their care.

When President Bill Clinton took office in 1993, managed care plans were also experiencing growth in expenditures (though at a slower rate) that private plans had witnessed previously. Clinton tried to arrest the rising costs and address some consumer concerns by proposing that managed care organizations compete in a market that would be regulated by the federal government. The hope was that competition would force HMOs and the like to offer more patient-friendly options while suppressing costs to be more attractive to employers and consumers. Clinton's plan, however, found no support from the health care industry or consumers, both of which disliked the notion of government regulation (though for different reasons).

In the wake of the failed Clinton plan, the various managed care organizations across the country coalesced into a few giants of the industry. These corporations made significant sums of money by pocketing the difference between the insurance premiums and the actual costs of medical care, which they were able to negotiate downward by applying pressure on doctors and providers to keep expenses low. State governments further added to the profits when they began contracting with large managed care corporations to help reduce the overall costs of Medicaid, the state and federal government health service for low-income and other disadvantaged groups.

Like the private sector, the federal government and state governments were experiencing rising health care expenditures. While the states battled with the costs of Medicaid, the federal government tried to stem costs in Medicare, the government insurance for retired or disabled workers. In 1997 Congress adopted the Medicare+Choice program to allow patients to choose from a variety of health plans offered by managed care insurers that might provide more desirable benefits (such as drug coverage) than could be obtained under standard Medicare. Many Medicare recipients, however, disliked the HMO plans (again because of being forced to find service within a network), and the HMO providers did not find it economical to service Medicare recipients (who use three times the medical provisions as non-Medicare recipients). With loss of interest on both sides, the number of Medicare HMO providers soon dwindled and the ranks of higher-cost, traditional Medicare plans swelled again.

When George W. Bush was elected president in 2000, he began looking at ways to reduce the costs of Medicare and halt the escalating growth of health care across the nation. In 2003, he signed into law the Medicare Prescription Drug, Improvement, and Modernization Act to add a prescription drug benefit (limiting drug costs) to Medicare recipients. The bill, the largest expansion to Medicare since its inception in 1965, allowed Medicare to contract with managed care organizations to offer the new benefit. The act also revamped Medicare+Choice (renamed Medicare Advantage) to give recipients more managed care choices, such as the implementation of Preferred Provider Organizations (which are similar to HMOs but patients can usually see any doctor they choose if they are willing to pay a slightly higher co-payment). Furthermore, the managed care providers are given government subsidies to offer more care options to the patients.

The act went into effect in 2006, but eager Medicare recipients began opting out of original Medicare insurance (which has a limited outpatient drug benefit) to take advantage of the greater variety of drug coverage and more health care options under the managed care plans. Critics believe the subsidies are too costly and that the managed care organizations may again drop coverage as the cost of paying for Medicare recipients mounts. They also contend that the law has no cost guarantees, so prices of drugs could affect premiums. The nonprofit women's health collective Our Bodies Ourselves warns that "seniors could ultimately end up paying more than we do today for medications." Our Bodies Ourselves concludes that "the program is designed to draw or even force seniors out of Medicare as we know it and into competing private health insurance plans."

After his success in pushing through the Medicare Prescription Drug, Improvement, and Modernization Act, President Bush set his sights on combating the national health crisis that was still exhibiting soaring costs and leaving many American families unsecured. In January 2007 he proposed to reform the taxing of health care by affording every American a tax deduction for purchasing health services (previously only those who had employer insurance enjoyed such a tax break because the wages used to contribute to employer plans were not counted as taxable income). The deduction would take effect by ignoring taxes on income that was used for health care—up to $15,000 per year for families and up to $7,500 for individuals. In addition, the president favors the expansion of health savings accounts (HSAs) to help deal with the high price of insurance. HSAs are personal accounts that are funded by individuals (and their employers, typically) and accrue interest over time. Individuals purchase a low-cost, high-deductible insurance policy to protect themselves against major illnesses, but they fund the HSA and draw on its balance to pay for smaller medical expenses. President Bush wants the HSAs to be given the tax breaks afforded to employer-based insurance, and he wants there to be less of a restriction on the amount of tax-free dollars that can be put into the account per year.

Overall, the president expects that by offering more tax breaks and eliminating the need for high-priced insurance, more Americans without insurance will have incentive and the financial ability to afford coverage. Steve Chapman, writing for the *Chicago Tribune*, argues that Bush's plan has two conspicuous virtues: "One is that it would increase the number of Americans with health insurance. The other is that it would build on the existing system rather than abandon it for one dominated by the federal government." The concept of government control is the element that doomed the Clinton plan. Critics charge, however, that sticking with the existing system is not going to help the health care crisis. Health care consultant and editorialist Matthew Holt suggests that those young people who have few medical expenditures will likely jump into HSAs. In the online news organ *Spot On*, he writes, "You can expect young employees to go [to] their employers and demand a few thousand dollars more in cash and then opt out of the health insurance benefit, and take the full tax deduction." This, he points out would leave the sicker, more needy employees stuck in an insurance market in which their greater demand on health services will drive up rates. Eventually, Holt writes, employers will dump their plans because of expense and tell employees to "go fend for themselves in the individual market." These cast-outs, who could never save enough in HSAs because of their continual need for health services, would then become uninsured or underinsured.

In an era of rising health care costs, obtaining health insurance of any kind is a challenge for many Americans. In a 2007 survey report, the Kaiser Family Foundation, a major health care policy research organization, states that "Seven in ten (70%) uninsured adults say that cost is the main reason they are uninsured." Another large percentage of Americans are underinsured, meaning their health care costs are consuming a significant part of their earnings. In the same report, Kaiser finds that "Nearly one-quarter (23%) of adults report problems paying medical bills within the past year, and more than six in ten of these (61%) have health insurance." Whether President Bush's tax break proposition will help the 47 million Americans without insurance is unknown. Congress has yet to approve the tax relief plan, and commentators can only guess at how popular such a plan would be with consumers.

One plan to ensure the right to coverage for all Americans—regardless of health, age, or employment—would be for the nation to adopt national health insurance. While the president's plan attempts, as Steve Chapman noted, tries to redress inequities within the system, many Americans—including several presidential hopefuls vying for candidacy during the 2008 election—are urging the government to pay for the county's health care needs. Most other developed nations have already made health care a national entitlement, and supporters wonder why the United States has not followed suit. They assert that national health care would eliminate insurance processing fees and paperwork expenses, thus lowering the cost. Opponents, on the other hand, contend that government control of nationalized services has always led to more bureaucracy and inefficiency that has never lowered costs or improved performance. Though national health insurance has been the subject of political debate for decades, the country has always opted to retain the current private-insurer system. A change of hands in the White House, however, might bring an end to the status quo.

In *Opposing Viewpoints: Health Care*, authors such as 2008 presidential hopeful Barack Obama argue for the adoption of national health insurance. Other politicians and commentators in this anthology—including President Bush—advocate for making changes within the current system in hopes that more people will be able to access the quality health care America possesses. In chapters entitled Is America's Health Care System in Need of Reform? How Should National Health Care Be Restructured? How Should the Current National

Health Care System Be Altered to Help the Uninsured? and How Should State Health Care Programs Be Altered? observers and critics such as Obama and Bush offer various strategies to reform health care to make it more affordable for the millions who still struggle to meet its high costs.

CHAPTER 1

Is America's Health Care System in Need of Reform?

Chapter Preface

The majority of critics of the U.S. health care system assert that it is wasteful and ineffectively organized. Bureaucracy and paperwork are blamed for delays in administering timely care and for consuming a large percentage of health costs; physicians and hospitals are charged with ordering unneeded tests or prescribing expensive drugs when generic alternatives are available; health insurers are accused of reaping huge profits from inflated pricing; and even the uninsured are held responsible for adding to high costs by utilizing medical services without picking up the bill. Whether there is truth in these accusations or not, health care costs in America have risen and so has the number of uninsured.

In August 2007 the U.S. Census Bureau reported that the number of Americans without health insurance increased by 2.2 million in the period between 2005 and 2006. The Kaiser Family Foundation and other leading health care analysis organizations claim that the rise is because many employers, faced with high costs of insurance, are dropping coverage for their workers. Other employers are instituting "defined contribution" health plans, which means that they will contribute a fixed amount to a specific health plan—regardless of the premium cost—and expect employees to pay the rest. This has led to a situation in which many working people are not uninsured but still are underinsured because they cannot always meet the high out-of-pocket expenses associated with employer health plans that shift costs to the employees.

Many American workers are finding it difficult to bear an increased burden of health costs. The National Coalition on Health Care states that health care expenses are now rising at nearly five times the rate of general inflation while workers' wages are not experiencing significant growth. The Department of Health and Human Services' Agency for Healthcare

Research and Quality reported that the percentage of Americans under age 65 whose family-level out-of-pocket spending for health care and insurance exceeds $2,000 a year rose by 16 percent between 1996 and 2003 (from 37.3 percent to 43.1 percent); those whose out-of-pocket spending for family health care exceeded $5,000 a year witnessed a 57 percent increase (from 9.1 percent to 14.3 percent) over the same period. For America's elderly, expenses are also high. According to the National Center for Policy Analysis, "seniors spend 17.2 percent of their cash incomes on health care, on the average, including out-of-pocket expenditures, as well as premiums for Medicare and individually purchased Medigap insurance."

In the following chapter, authors debate whether these expenses and their connection to the swelling ranks of the uninsured are cause for a restructuring of the health care system in America. While some see the problems as a serious indictment of the current system's failures, others put forth the notion that Americans cannot put too lean a price on health care—especially when the care received is, in their view, of the highest quality in the world.

> *"By 2010, inflation-adjusted government health care spending is projected to grow to an average of $13,000 per household."*

Health Care Spending Is out of Control

Eugene Steuerle

Eugene Steuerle is a senior fellow at the Urban Institute, a public policy think-tank that evaluates civic programs and services affecting urban populations and American society as a whole. In the following viewpoint, Steuerle states that since 1975, health care spending in America has doubled and is expected to double again by the year 2016. He worries that rising costs are consuming huge portions of the federal budget (that pay for subsidies and government health programs), leaving Congress little opportunity to allocate tax revenues to other federal programs. Steuerle maintains that such monies might be better spent on preventative health programs that would reduce the demand for chronic disease management and expensive health care treatments.

As you read, consider the following questions:

1. As Steuerle relates, what percentage of health expenditures in 2006 was consumed by Medicare alone?
2. What does the author say is the largest federal tax break?
3. How do tax subsidies "drive up" the cost of health care, according to Steuerle?

Since 1975, total spending on health care in the United States has doubled, and it now comprises one-sixth of the U.S. economy, or about $2.2 trillion. By 2016, some projections show total health spending almost doubling to $4.1 trillion and consuming one-fifth of the nation's gross domestic product.

Much of the increase in health costs has been paid for through direct government expenditures and tax subsidies. The government's role in financing health care is also growing due to the recent Medicare expansion. The budget for health care will likely grow more than any other area of government [in 2007]. Recent Congressional Budget Office estimates show that the majority of the projected $344 billion increase in federal revenues in 2010—relative to 2006 and absent additional revenues lost to tax subsidies for health—is scheduled to go automatically to cover the cost of additional health expenditures and the revenues lost to tax subsidies for health.

Current Government Health Care Spending

Government health programs (principally Medicare and Medicaid) and tax subsidies accounted for more than half ($1.3 trillion) of total health expenditures in 2006. Government statistics also reveal:

- In 2006, total health care spending averaged $19,000 per household; about 58 percent of the total, or

$11,000 per household, was in the form of government-subsidized health care;

- By 2010, inflation-adjusted government health care spending is projected to grow to an average of $13,000 per household;

- Health care will climb to 25.8 percent of total government outlays in 2008 and 28.4 percent in 2012.

The majority of growth in government spending on health care is due to Medicare:

- Medicare accounted for 38 percent of public spending on health care in 2005, and it has grown an average of 9.3 percent annually since 2002;

- The cost per beneficiary (Medicare and Medicaid) has continually been increasing faster than the per capita growth of the economy, and the Medicare actuaries see no end in sight.

Congress has attempted to cut reimbursements for Medicare providers, and the growth of Medicare was projected to slow to 6.5 percent [in 2007]. However, legislators have already reversed the cuts in physician payments for 2007, so the actual growth rate may be higher.

Tax Breaks Raise Costs

Health care spending has also grown because of tax subsidies. Tax subsidies lower the private cost of health care, but they raise the total public cost in the sense that these revenues could have been spent elsewhere. The income tax break for employer-provided health insurance alone is the largest federal tax break, and it is also the largest health subsidy in the tax or expenditure systems for the nonelderly and nondisabled. The federal government also subsidizes employer-provided insurance through a Social Security tax break, and state governments forgo income tax revenues as well. In sum, more than $250 billion in revenues each year are forgone due to tax subsidies for health insurance. These subsidies are open-ended; according to one estimate, the cost of tax preferences for health insurance will grow by $58 billion in 2010.

These tax breaks are not very efficient at expanding health care, nor are they distributed equitably. They tend to favor people with higher incomes, those with more expensive health plans and those living in areas with higher-than-average utilization of services to treat the same problems treated elsewhere. The exclusion of employer-provided health benefits from wages sometimes reduces the taxes of higher-income households as much as $3,000 or more, while many moderate-income taxpayers only get one-half or one-fourth of that amount—and sometimes nothing at all.

By any standard, taxpayers are not getting their money's worth: Instead of buying coverage for more people, the subsidies encourage insured people to buy higher-cost insurance, which encourages more use of high-cost health care and ultimately drives up health costs. Rising health care costs leads to more expensive insurance. Many individuals and employers simply will not pay those high insurance costs. Thus, in the end, the *incremental amounts* spent each year may actually be increasing—yes, increasing, not decreasing—the number of uninsured!

Money That Could Be Better Spent

Large automatic growth in expenditures only for certain programs leaves Congress in a straightjacket, with little flexibility to determine how to allocate additional revenues to meet the most important needs of the nation. As the share of spending on health grows, the share scheduled for many other programs, such as education and children's programs, is scheduled to decline.

How Future Increases in Revenue Have Already Been Spent on Health Care: 2010 versus 2006

current law, 2006 dollars

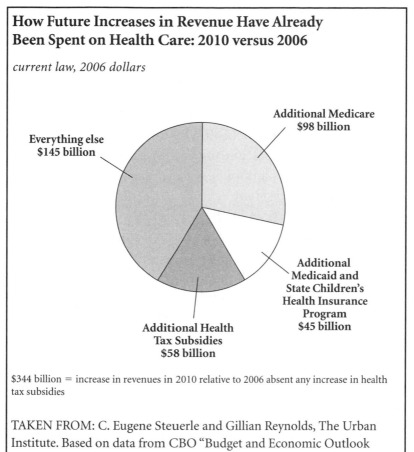

Additional Medicare
$98 billion

Everything else
$145 billion

Additional
Medicaid and
State Children's
Health Insurance
Program
$45 billion

Additional Health
Tax Subsidies
$58 billion

$344 billion = increase in revenues in 2010 relative to 2006 absent any increase in health tax subsidies

TAKEN FROM: C. Eugene Steuerle and Gillian Reynolds, The Urban Institute. Based on data from CBO "Budget and Economic Outlook 2008–2010" and Analytical Perspectives FY2007. Table 19.1.

Within health care itself, two or three years' worth of Medicare growth could pay for a decent health insurance package for all children, and a few years' worth of growth in health insurance tax subsidies, which mainly benefit higher-earning employees, could pay for a modest health insurance tax credit for households at all income levels. Furthermore, the growth of government spending on existing health programs and tax subsidies consumes resources that might otherwise go toward achieving higher immunization rates, enhancing services for the frail elderly, expanding preventive care or increasing the budget of the Centers for Disease Control and Prevention.

Every year, billions more are spent on health care in the United States. Most of the additional revenues generated through economic growth are now scheduled to go toward costs in existing health programs, regardless of their effectiveness in meeting the nation's health and nonhealth needs. The government's portion of spending is growing especially fast because most government health benefits are not appropriated: Spending increases automatically each year without a vote by Congress. This autopilot feature means that even when Congress and the president "cut" a little here or there from the discretionary portion of the budget, the mandatory government health care spending trajectory usually overwhelms any saving achieved. The important question is whether past government tax and spending policies can be taken off autopilot and redirected to fairly and efficiently meet the nation's needs, including the health care needs, of Americans today and tomorrow.

"Advances in medical technology have generated a lot of value. As a consequence, it is no surprise that we are spending more on health care."

Health Care Spending Has Value

Martin Gaynor and Deepti Gudipati

In the following viewpoint, Martin Gaynor and Deepti Gudipati argue that rising health care costs are offset by coinciding advances in medicine. Because these advances have improved quality of life and generally increased human longevity, they have value, the authors assert, and therefore they are worth the expenditure. Still, Gaynor and Gudipati agree with critics who claim that the large portion of money spent on health care could be decreased in order to pay for other beneficial government programs. Martin Gaynor is a professor of economics and health policy at the Heinz School at Carnegie Mellon University. Deepti Gudipati is a graduate student in public policy and management at the university.

Martin Gaynor, Deepti Gudipati, "Health Care Costs: Do We Need a Cure?" *Heinz School Review*, vol. 3, November 5, 2006. © 2006 The Heinz School Review. Reproduced by permission. http://journal.heinz.cmu.edu.

As you read, consider the following questions:

1. According to the authors, by what percent did the mortality rate from heart disease fall between 1980 and 2002?

2. What are some of the "distortions" that the authors say are adding to the inefficient way in which health care money is spent?

3. What are the two problems associated with restraining health care costs in America, in Gaynor and Gudipati's view?

U.S. health care spending is high and rising rapidly. The U.S. spent $1.9 trillion on health care, or $6,280 per person, in 2004. Health spending rose 7.9 percent in 2004, and the health spending share of GDP grew 0.1 percentage point, to 16.0 percent in 2004, making health care the largest industry in the U.S. economy. Spending on health care is rising faster than the overall growth in the economy. We now spend more on health care than on food, clothing, computer hardware and software, or national defense. Not surprisingly, health insurance premiums are also increasing, along with concerns about the burden of mounting health care costs on individuals and society.

Health care costs are indeed very high and growing rapidly. But, so what? From one perspective, this is not a problem at all, but a good thing. How so? Let's use simple economic reasoning to frame our thinking. When should we be spending an increasing share of income on something? The answer is that we should spend more when that good is increasing in value. When should we spend a large share of income on a good or service? We should when that good generates a lot of value.

Advances in Medicine Reduce Mortality Rates

It is certainly the case that there have been major advances in medical technology. We are much better at treating heart disease, cancer, and other life-threatening conditions. The mortality rate from heart disease fell by over 40 percent from 1980 to 2002, and the death rate from cancer fell by 7 percent over the same period. Another important indicator of health is the infant mortality rate, which fell by 47 percent from 1980-2002. Overall, life expectancy at birth in the United States has increased by 10 years since 1950 (78 vs. 68 years), 5 years since 1980, and by 2 years since only 1995.

In addition, there have been major advances in treating conditions that are not life threatening, but have a major impact on quality of life. Problems of severe mental illness, such as schizophrenia and depression, can be treated very effectively with modern medications, so much so that many patients can live normal, productive lives. Orthopedic problems can now be treated so that patients with severe problems recover nearly complete functioning. Degraded knee or hip joints can be replaced with artificial ones, and patients can resume active lives. Cataracts can now be removed and replaced with an artificial lens in a quick, simple outpatient procedure using only a topical anesthetic and without the use of stitches. Recovery is fast and vision can even be improved beyond what it was before the onset of cataracts. Many surgical procedures that once required large openings can now be done with laparoscopes, which only require small incisions. As a consequence recovery times are substantially shorter, as is the risk of infection.

The Economics of Health Spending

These advances are extraordinary. While the values of non-life-threatening advances have not yet been estimated, economists have estimated the value of increased life expectancy.

Economists Kevin Murphy and Robert Topel (2005) have valued the increases in life expectancy between 1970 and 2000 at about $3.2 trillion per year, an amount equal to about one-half of average annual national income over the period. [Economists] David Cutler and Mark McClellan (2001) estimate that every dollar spent on the treatment of heart disease has generated 7 dollars worth of value to society, and every dollar spent on treating low birthweight infants has generated 6 dollars worth of value for us.

What this tells us is that advances in medical technology have generated a lot of value. As a consequence, it is no surprise that we are spending more on health care. In fact, there is strong evidence to indicate that increases in health spending have been substantially outweighed by the value of increased life expectancy.

So growth in health spending appears to have been "worth it" on average. This leaves us with 2 questions. Has the growth in health spending been worth it on the margin? And what about the level of health spending—are we spending too much in absolute terms?

Are Americans Spending Too Much?

The question about whether the growth in spending has been worth it on the margin is a question about whether the last dollar of this increased spending generated at least a dollar's worth of value. Economists agree that the growth in health spending has been driven by advances in medical technology, so this is a question about whether the additional spending on these innovations has generated at least as much additional value to society. The answer to this is unclear. We do not have direct evidence on this question; however, some theories suggest that we may actually have too little innovation, due to imperfections in the health care system.

There is a reason to worry about growing spending on health care, however, and that is its effect on the federal bud-

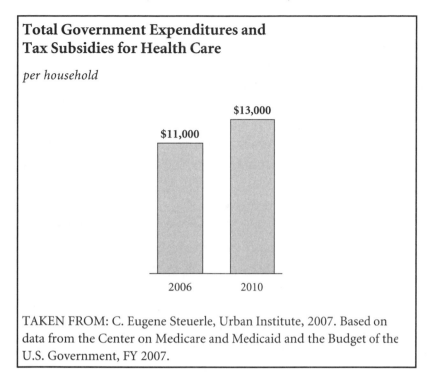

Total Government Expenditures and Tax Subsidies for Health Care

per household

$13,000

$11,000

2006   2010

TAKEN FROM: C. Eugene Steuerle, Urban Institute, 2007. Based on data from the Center on Medicare and Medicaid and the Budget of the U.S. Government, FY 2007.

get. Approximately one-half of all U.S. health care spending is financed by the government, most of it through the federal Medicare and Medicaid programs. High Medicare and Medicaid costs must be financed through budget deficits, higher taxes, or cuts in federal programs. Our large and growing federal budget deficit is, at present, largely financed by foreign investors. However, it seems unlikely that this can continue indefinitely without serious adverse effects on the economy. Continuing increases in government spending on health care are therefore not likely sustainable without serious macroeconomic consequences.

What about the level of health care costs—are we spending too much? Here the answer is probably "yes." We'd probably be better off if we spent a few dollars less on health care and allocated resources to some other uses (addressing global warming, improving national security, providing better education for low-income areas, etc.), or reallocated the current level of health care spending from some current uses to other types of care that are higher valued. The reason is that our health care system is subject to quite a few distortions. The design of insurance policies (both private and public), market power, policies for paying doctors and hospitals, asymmetric information, and government subsidies and regulations are all present in health care markets and combine to distort the functioning of the health care system. As a result, some of our health care spending is inefficient.

It is worth pointing out that there are distributional aspects associated with health care spending. The burden of increased private health care spending is borne nearly entirely by workers, not health insurers or employers. Research evidence shows that a dollar increase in health insurance costs for employers is paid for by workers, either by one dollar of pay they don't get, or by a reduction in health benefits, including no insurance. The number of people in the U.S. without any health insurance at all stood at 46.6 million, or 15.9% of the population, in 2005. This number has been increased by 6 million people since 2000.

Reducing Expenditure Without Reducing Value

So what is to be done? While there are some good reasons to worry about health care spending, it must be recognized that a great deal of this spending has generated value. We are living longer and living better, and that's worth a great deal. Nonetheless, we need to find a way to rationally restrain health care costs. This will be a difficult task.

There are two problems associated with accomplishing this task. The first problem is the usual one: "no pain, no gain." While we are probably spending too much on health care, most of that spending is generating value for those who are using and providing it. These individuals are unlikely to readily

The Value of Fighting Mortality

Prospectively, even modest progress against mortality-causing diseases such as cancer and heart disease would have enormous social values. A 1 percent reduction in mortality from cancer or heart disease would be worth nearly $500 billion to current and future Americans. These estimates ignore the value of health advances to individuals in other countries, so they likely understate aggregate social values of possible innovations. They also ignore corresponding improvements in the quality of life—which evidence suggests may be even more valuable than gains in longevity—and for these reasons as well, they are likely to be conservative. We show that these values will increase in the future because of economic growth and, more interestingly, because health itself continues to improve.

Kevin M. Murphy and Robert H. Topel,
"The Value of Health and Longevity,"
National Bureau of Economic Research Working Paper No. 11405,
June 2005.

agree to policies that deprive them of care that they find privately beneficial. The second problem is finding a way to reduce spending on things that are generating little additional benefit relative to cost, without reducing spending on things that are highly beneficial. In particular, it is important to avoid reducing spending on beneficial innovations.

This will be a key challenge for health care policy. Reducing health care spending will be difficult, and the temptation will be to reduce health care spending across the board. This is a temptation to be avoided. Cutting spending unilaterally will decrease the good with the bad, and will constrain valuable innovations. Policymakers will need to take care to ensure that the cure isn't worse than the disease.

> "It is true that Americans spend more per capita for health care and that is because they get more health care per capita."

The United States Has One of the Best Health Care Systems

James Peron

James Peron argues in the following viewpoint that Americans spend a great deal on health care because they receive more health care benefits than most other countries—especially those with socialized medicine. The cost of health care in the United States is expensive, Peron maintains, because doctors use the best technologies and medical advances to meet the demands of their patients. Peron expects that competition in the medical field will help reduce the exploding cost of health care, not the implementation of socialized medicine, which would only ration care and deny the best services to many patients in need. James Peron is the author of Zimbabwe: Death of a Dream *and several other books. He has written for various newspapers including the* Wall Street Journal *(Europe) and is the editor of the book* The Liberal Tide: From Tyranny to Liberty.

James Peron, "The Illusion of Socialized Health Care," *Classically Liberal Web Log*, January 18, 2007. Reproduced by permission of the author. http://freestudents.blog spot.com.

As you read, consider the following questions:

1. In Peron's view, why does the "inexactness" of prescribing health care contribute to increased costs?
2. What is the effect of underspending in nations with state-run health care, in Peron's view?
3. In the example that Peron relates, how did South Africa's free health care for children program fail the people?

Americans spend more per capita on automobiles than do Nigerians. Is there an American car crisis? Americans spend more per capita on houses than do Chinese. Is there an American house crisis? If you look at American per capita spending on various goods, you will often find that Americans spend more per capita than many other nations, if not more per capita than most nations.

Films, cosmetics, computers, cars, houses, pets, magazines, chocolate, the list is almost endless. If you take these items and compare per capita spending on them to the spending in other nations, you will regularly find America in the lead.

But you don't hear people talking about the chocolate crisis, the pet food crisis, the lipstick crisis, etc. We don't do that because spending more is not necessarily a bad thing. If individual B spends $500 a year on cosmetics while individual C spends $0, that doesn't mean that C is better off. It may mean that C can't afford any cosmetics while B is well off. This is true for every consumer good you can think of, including health care.

Backward Socialist Thinking

But when it comes to health care, the advocates of socialist systems of care immediately reverse things. Americans are worse off because they spend more. And that is true. Americans spend more because they purchase more. The average American receives more health care than the average European.

The assumption in much of the world is that American health care is significantly inferior because Americans spend more per person than do people in other wealthy nations.

But no health care system anywhere in the world has been able to make health care available to everyone. Every state provider of care restricts services, often through the use of queuing. Canada's health care is lauded by advocates of state systems, yet Canadians wait significant periods of time for what care is available. One factor often ignored is that most Canadians live along the US border and that some of the [health care] for Canadians is provided privately in the United States.

There is little argument that American health care is among the best in the world when it comes to technologies and innovation. What is targeted for criticism is that costs are high and this restricts access.

Improved Technology Raises Costs

Economist Arnold Kling points out in his book *Crisis of Abundance* that in the last 30 years very highly sophisticated new medical procedures have been developed. And these are extremely expensive in themselves. Health care costs in the American government's budget are a problem. But Kling notes, that if the same sort of care available in 1975 were what was available today, the budget would be safe. New technologies have driven up cost considerably. Costs have gone up because more expensive new technologies push up those costs. Many socialist systems don't have that problem because they decline to use the technology or severely restrict access to it.

Other nations ration these expensive technologies in ways that American consumers find unacceptable. And Kling suggests that this rationing has "also slowed the adoption of premium medicine" where practised.

An Example of Government Rationing in Britain

[In 2004] many British hospitals stopped providing heart bypass surgery to smokers. The waiting lists were so long that they wanted to give priority to non-smokers who responded better to surgery. [In 2005] several regions stopped providing knee and hip replacements to overweight patients because their response to surgery was not as favorable as thin patients on the waiting lists. [In 2006] the *British Medical Journal* reports that physicians in the National Health Service are often no longer treating patients age 80 or over for strokes.

Richard E. Ralston, Americans for Free Choice in Medicine, September 19, 2006. www.afcm.org.

These premium services do raise the cost of health care. And, as Kling notes, health care is not an exact science. Often a physician looks at a problem, tries his best to determine causes and takes actions which may, or may not, help. He has to make educated guesses but often still guesses none the less. With so many people ready to sue physicians for making the wrong educated guess, it is in the benefit of physicians to take all reasonable precautions regardless of cost. A headache could be just a headache solved by a few cents worth of aspirin, or it could be something far more serious requiring tests costing hundreds of dollars just to rule out that possibility. Before the invention of such techniques the recommendation may well have been "Take two aspirins and call me in the morning." Physicians may well be penalized today if they don't over test.

Americans Want the Best Care

Care is often provided by ruling out problems. A patient has specific symptoms which may indicate a number of problems.

The physician begins to narrow down the options. Different problems require different solutions and what may work for one problem may make another worse. But imagine if no tests were available for this winnowing process. More patients would suffer from having their problems continue, but health care costs would be significantly lower.

Today in the US there are about 25 million MRI [magnetic resonance imaging] scans performed per year. In 1990 it was 1.8 million and none were performed in 1980. This cost didn't exist in the 80s because the technology didn't exist. Abolishing new technologies would lower health care costs significantly. But people would suffer and there would be more deaths—but it would be cheaper.

Today people want the best care that money can buy. That is the problem. New technologies come onto the market daily. These are often capital intensive services requiring highly skilled care givers. The physician of the old days, that some yearn for, could still exist provided patients are willing to accept the care provided in the old days. But they can't have it both ways.

American consumers are facing higher medical costs due to procedures that are not as available in state-care systems. Kling notes: "Heart bypass surgery is about three times as prevalent [in the US] as in France and about twice as prevalent as in the U.K. Angioplasty is more than twice as prevalent . . . as in France and about seven times as prevalent as in the U.K." And what is true for technology is true for personnel. America has the highest rate of medical specialists in the world. All this premium health care does make health care in total more expensive in the US than elsewhere. This is what Kling calls the "Crisis of Abundance."

The Problem of Third-Party Payment

Is America overspending on health care? No doubt. But it is also likely that state systems are under spending as well. The extra money that Americans spend is one reason there aren't queues for surgery. Clearly the third party payment system in the US has driven up costs through the use of premium care. But equally clear is that state systems attempt to reduce this tendency to over consume by rationing care. No central planner can ration health care in a way that optimizes care for all patients. They paint with a wide brush and that means needed care is not given and what is given often is in such short supply that patients die before they move to the top of the waiting list.

America is said to have a health care crisis because it spends more than any other nation per capita. But Americans also lead the world in spending on food, entertainment and automobiles. Yet no one speaks of the food crisis, entertainment crisis or automobile crisis. Of course the big difference is that Americans don't have their food, cars or entertainment paid for by a third party such as insurance or government.

Some health costs were due to the explosion in demand for services, not due to increased illness. They were the result of the rise of new methods of paying for services. Mostly the patient was put into a situation where he did not pay directly for the costs of his visit. Approximately 86% of health care costs for Americans is paid for by either government or insurance. This is actually higher than the coverage given under Canada's state system.

One result of such high third party payments is that demand for care goes up, which increases per capita costs as well.

Competition Reduces Costs

Now patients are starting to pay a fairer share of these costs themselves. One result has been increased competition in health care and improved health services. The *New York Times* recently reported that in the US a "growing number of physicians ... have streamlined their schedules and added Internet services, among other steps, to better meet the needs of patients. For physicians . . . it is simply good business."

The reason for the improved services is that in recent years, walk-in medical clinics and retail-store clinics have dramatically increased and "pose new competition, and as shrinking insurance benefits mean patients are paying more of their own bills, family care medicine is more than ever a consumer-service business. And it pays to keep the customer satisfied."

Socialized Medicine Fails Other Countries

In South Africa, the government announced "free" health care for children under a certain age. How was that provided? One was by neglecting other patients who needed care. A second thing they did was arbitrarily limit that care to certain infants only. For instance, if the birth weight was below a certain weight, the child was denied life saving care even if it were available.

In one case a mother was told that the hospital would not save her infant's life even though it had the ability to do so. It was a few grams below the weight limit set by the state. Press reports on the case brought in private donations; the mother and infant moved to a private hospital and the baby lived.

In England a winner of the Big Brother reality show was asked what he planned to do with his large cash winning. He said that a big chunk of it was earmarked to fly a friend to the United States for badly needed surgery. The surgery could be done in England, but the socialist system refused to do it because it cost too much. Britain spends less per capita on health care than America does and denying needed surgeries like this is one reason. Deny people needed health care by bureaucratic edict and you can lower the costs per capita.

There is no denying that Americans consume more health care than they need. That is what third party payment schemes do. Nor can anyone deny that some Americans get less health care than they need. But the same is true in socialist systems.

There are many people who over consume on small issues because the state covers the costs but who under consume on big issues because the state won't provide the care at all.

America could match the other developed nations in per capita spending Tomorrow, but to do so it would have to do what they have done—deny certain expensive treatments across the board.

> "The U.S. health system is the most expensive in the world, but comparative analyses consistently show the United States underperforms relative to other countries on most dimensions of performance."

The United States Does Not Have One of the Best Health Care Systems

Karen Davis et al.

In the following viewpoint, economist Karen Davis and colleagues analyze five criteria related to the quality of health care services in the United States and other nations with high-performance health care. Based on their findings, Davis and her colleagues conclude that the United States is underperforming, trailing its counterparts in patient access to health care and equity of service to different socioeconomic classes. Since Americans pay significantly more for health care than other nations, the authors insist that the United States needs to improve its standings to provide a better value for the price. Karen Davis is the president of the Commonwealth Fund, a philanthropic organization

Karen Davis et al., "Mirror, Mirror on the Wall: An International Update on the Comparative Performance of American Health Care," *The Commonwealth Fund*, May 15, 2007. Copyright © 2007 The Commonwealth Fund. Reproduced by permission.

that analyzes health and social policy issues. The six coauthors who aided in the drafting of this viewpoint are also members of the Commonwealth Fund.

As you read, consider the following questions:

1. Who provided the survey data on which the Commonwealth Fund rankings were based?

2. What was the most notable distinction between the United States and other countries in the Commonwealth Fund rankings, according to Davis and colleagues?

3. How do information technologies in other countries help better their health care responses?

Despite having the most costly health system in the world, the United States consistently underperforms on most dimensions of performance, relative to other countries. This report—an update to two earlier editions—includes data from surveys of patients, as well as information from primary care physicians about their medical practices and views of their countries' health systems. Compared with five other nations—Australia, Canada, Germany, New Zealand, the United Kingdom—the U.S. health care system ranks last or next-to-last on five dimensions of a high performance health system: quality, access, efficiency, equity, and healthy lives. The U.S. is the only country in the study without universal health insurance coverage, partly accounting for its poor performance on access, equity, and health outcomes. The inclusion of physician survey data also shows the U.S. lagging in adoption of information technology and use of nurses to improve care coordination for the chronically ill.

The United States Continually Lags Behind Other Nations

The U.S. health system is the most expensive in the world, but comparative analyses consistently show the United States underperforms relative to other countries on most dimensions of performance. This report, which includes information from primary care physicians about their medical practices and views of their countries' health systems, confirms the patient survey findings discussed in previous editions of *Mirror, Mirror*. It also includes information on health care outcomes that were featured in the U.S. health system scorecard issued by the Commonwealth Fund Commission on a High Performance Health System.

Among the six nations studied—Australia, Canada, Germany, New Zealand, the United Kingdom, and the United States—the U.S. ranks last, as it did in the 2006 and 2004 editions of *Mirror, Mirror*. Most troubling, the U.S. fails to achieve better health outcomes than the other countries, and as shown in the earlier editions, the U.S. is last on dimensions of access, patient safety, efficiency, and equity. The 2007 edition includes data from the six countries and incorporates patients' and physicians' survey results on care experiences and ratings on various dimensions of care.

Lack of Universal Health Care

The most notable way the U.S. differs from other countries is the absence of universal health insurance coverage. Other nations ensure the accessibility of care through universal health insurance systems and through better ties between patients and the physician practices that serve as their long-term "medical home." It is not surprising, therefore, that the U.S. substantially underperforms other countries on measures of access to care and equity in health care between populations with above-average and below average incomes.

With the inclusion of physician survey data in the analysis, it is also apparent that the U.S. is lagging in adoption of information technology and national policies that promote quality improvement. The U.S. can learn from what physicians and patients have to say about practices that can lead to better management of chronic conditions and better coordination of care. Information systems in countries like Germany, New Zealand, and the U.K. enhance the ability of physicians to monitor chronic conditions and medication use. These countries also routinely employ non-physician clinicians such as nurses to assist with managing patients with chronic diseases.

The area where the U.S. health care system performs best is preventive care, an area that has been monitored closely for over a decade by managed care plans. Nonetheless, the U.S. scores particularly poorly on its ability to promote healthy lives, and on the provision of care that is safe and coordinated, as well as accessible, efficient, and equitable.

For all countries, responses indicate room for improvement. Yet, the other five countries spend considerably less on health care per person and as a percent of gross domestic product than does the United States. These findings indicate that, from the perspectives of both physicians and patients, the U.S. health care system could do much better in achieving better value for the nation's substantial investment in health.

Ranked Attributes

Quality The indicators of quality were grouped into four categories: right (or effective) care, safe care, coordinated care, and patient-centered care. Compared with the other five countries, the U.S. fares best on provision and receipt of preventive care, a dimension of "right care." However, its low scores on chronic care management and safe, coordinated, and patient-centered care pull its overall quality score down. Other countries are further along than the U.S. in using information technology and a team approach to manage chronic conditions and coordinate care. Information systems in countries like Germany, New Zealand, and the U.K. enhance the ability of physicians to identify and monitor patients with chronic conditions. Such systems also make it easy for physicians to

Overall Ranking

	Australia	Canada	Germany	New Zealand	United Kingdom	United States
Overall Ranking (2007)	3.5	5	2	3.5	1	6
Quality care	4	6	2.5	2.5	1	5
Right care	5	6	3	4	2	1
Safe care	4	5	1	3	2	6
Coordinated care	3	6	4	2	1	5
Patient-centered care	3	6	2	1	4	5
Access	3	5	1	2	4	6
Efficiency	4	5	3	2	1	6
Equity	2	5	4	3	1	6
Healthy lives	1	3	2	4.5	4.5	6
Health expenditures per capita, 2004	$2,876*	$3,165	$3,005*	$2,083	$2,546	$6,102

*2003 data

Country rankings

□ 1.00–2.66   □ 2.67–4.33   ■ 4.34–6.00

TAKEN FROM: Calculated by the Commonwealth Fund 2004 International Health Policy Survey, the Commonwealth Fund 2005 International Health Policy Survey of Sicker Adults, the 2006 Commonwealth Fund International Health Policy Survey of Primary Care Physicians, and the Commonwealth Fund Commission on a High Performance Health System National Scorecard.

print out medication lists, including those prescribed by other physicians. Nurses help patients manage their chronic diseases, with those services financed by governmental programs.

Access Not surprising—given the absence of universal coverage—people in the U.S. go without needed health care because of cost more often than people do in the other countries. Americans were the most likely to say they had access problems related to cost, but if insured, patients in the U.S. have rapid access to specialized health care services. In other countries, like the U.K and Canada, patients have little to no financial burden, but experience long wait times for such specialized services. The U.S. and Canada rank lowest on the prompt accessibility of appointments with physicians, with patients more likely to report waiting six or more days for an appointment when needing care. Germany scores well on patients' perceptions of access to care on nights and weekends and on the ability of primary care practices to make arrangements for patients to receive care when the office is closed. Overall, Germany ranks first on access.

Efficiency On indicators of efficiency, the U.S. ranks last among the six countries, with the U.K. and New Zealand ranking first and second, respectively. The U.S. has poor performance on measures of national health expenditures and administrative costs as well as on measures of the use of information technology and multidisciplinary teams. Also, of sicker respondents who visited the emergency room, those in Germany and New Zealand are less likely to have done so for a condition that could have been treated by a regular doctor, had one been available.

Equity The U.S. ranks a clear last on all measures of equity. Americans with below-average incomes were much more likely than their counterparts in other countries to report not visiting a physician when sick, not getting a recommended test, treatment or follow-up care, not filling a prescription, or not seeing a dentist when needed because of costs. On each of these indicators, more than two-fifths of lower-income adults in the U.S. said they went without needed care because of costs in the past year.

Healthy Lives The U.S. ranks last overall with poor scores on all three indicators of healthy lives. The U.S. and U.K. had much higher death rates in 1998 from conditions amenable to medical care—with rates 25 to 50 percent higher than Canada and Australia. Overall, Australia ranks highest on healthy lives, scoring first or second on all of the indicators.

Room for Improvement

Findings in this report confirm many of the findings from the earlier two editions of *Mirror, Mirror*. The U.S. ranks last of six nations overall. As in the earlier editions, the U.S. ranks last on indicators of patient safety, efficiency, and equity. New Zealand, Australia, and the U.K. continue to demonstrate superior performance, with Germany joining their ranks of top performers. The U.S. is first on preventive care, and second only to Germany on waiting times for specialist care and non-emergency surgical care, but weak on access to needed services and ability to obtain prompt attention from physicians.

Any attempt to assess the relative performance of countries has inherent limitations. These rankings summarize evidence on measures of high performance based on national mortality data and the perceptions and experiences of patients and physicians. They do not capture important dimensions of effectiveness or efficiency that might be obtained from medical records or administrative data. Patients' and physicians' assessments might be affected by their experiences and expectations, which could differ by country and culture.

The findings indicate room for improvement across all of the countries, especially in the U.S. If the health care system is to perform according to patients' expectations, the nation will need to remove financial barriers to care and improve the delivery of care. Disparities in terms of access to services signal the need to expand insurance to cover the uninsured and to ensure that all Americans have an accessible medical home. The U.S. must also accelerate its efforts to adopt health information technology and ensure an integrated medical record and information system that is accessible to providers and patients.

While many U.S. hospitals and health systems are dedicated to improving the process of care to achieve better safety and quality, the U.S. can also learn from innovations in other countries—including public reporting of quality data, payment systems that reward high-quality care, and a team approach to management of chronic conditions. Based on these patient and physician reports, the U.S. could improve the delivery, coordination, and equity of the health care system by drawing from best practices both within the U.S. and around the world.

"*Affordable, universal health care for every single American must not be a question of whether, it must be a question of how.*"

The United States Needs Universal Health Care

Barack Obama

Barack Obama is a U.S. Senator from Illinois and a contender for the democratic ticket in the 2008 presidential election. He serves on the Senate's Health, Education, Labor and Pensions Committee, which oversees America's health care, schools, employment, and retirement programs. In the following viewpoint, Obama states that America needs universal health care. He argues that rising costs have eaten away at the wages of those who can afford health care and have left millions unable to pay for basic insurance coverage. Obama contends that the nation needs bold leadership to bring about universal coverage, update obsolete technology, and figure out ways to reduce excessive costs borne under the current system.

Barack Obama, "The Time Has Come for Universal Health Care," speech at Families USA Conference, Washington, DC, January 25, 2007. http://obama.senate.gov.

As you read, consider the following questions:

1. What does Obama mean when he speaks about the "smallness" of American politics in relation to issues like health care reform?

2. Why can foreign automakers typically "run circles around" American counterparts, according to Obama?

3. How much do Obama and other members of Congress believe the U.S. could save per year if health records and other aspects of the health system were put online?

On this January morning of two thousand and seven, more than sixty years after President Harry Truman first issued the call for national health insurance, we find ourselves in the midst of an historic moment on health care. From Maine to California, from business to labor, from Democrats to Republicans, the emergence of new and bold proposals from across the spectrum has effectively ended the debate over whether or not we should have universal health care in this country.

Plans that tinker and halfway measures now belong to yesterday. [President George W. Bush's] latest proposal that does little to bring down cost or guarantee coverage falls into this category. There will be many others offered in the coming [2008 presidential] campaign, and I am working with experts to develop my own plan as we speak, but let's make one thing clear right here, right now:

> In the 2008 campaign, affordable, universal health care for every single American must not be a question of whether, it must be a question of how. We have the ideas, we have the resources, and we will have universal health care in this country by the end of the next president's first term.

I know there's a cynicism out there about whether this can happen, and there's reason for it. Every four years, health care plans are offered up in campaigns with great fanfare and promise. But once those campaigns end, the plans collapse under the weight of Washington politics, leaving the rest of America to struggle with skyrocketing costs.

Apathy in the Face of Needed Change

For too long, this debate has been stunted by what I call the smallness of our politics—the idea that there isn't much we can agree on or do about the major challenges facing our country. And when some try to propose something bold, the interests groups and the partisans treat it like a sporting event, with each side keeping score of who's up and who's down, using fear and divisiveness and other cheap tricks to win their argument, even if we lose our solution in the process.

Well we can't afford another disappointing charade in 2008. It's not only tiresome, it's wrong. Wrong when businesses have to lay off one employee because they can't afford the health care of another. Wrong when a parent cannot take a sick child to the doctor because they cannot afford the bill that comes with it. Wrong when 46 million Americans have no health care at all. In a country that spends more on health care than any other nation on Earth, it's just wrong.

And yet, in recent years, what's caught the attention of those who haven't always been in favor of reform is the realization that this crisis isn't just morally offensive, it's economically untenable. For years, the can't-do crowd has scared the American people into believing that universal health care would mean socialized medicine and burdensome taxes—that we should just stay out of the way and tinker at the margins.

You know the statistics. Family premiums are up by nearly 87% over the last five years, growing five times faster than workers' wages. Deductibles are up 50%. Co-payments for care and prescriptions are through the roof.

Nearly 11 million Americans who are already insured spent more than a quarter of their salary on health care last year. And over half of all family bankruptcies today are caused by medical bills.

But they say it's too costly to act.

Almost half of all small businesses no longer offer health care to their workers, and so many others have responded to rising costs by laying off workers or shutting their doors for good. Some of the biggest corporations in America, giants of industry like GM and Ford, are watching foreign competitors based in countries with universal health care run circles around them, with a GM car containing twice as much health care cost as a Japanese car.

But they say it's too risky to act.

They tell us it's too expensive to cover the uninsured, but they don't mention that every time an American without health insurance walks into an emergency room, we pay even more. Our family's premiums are $922 higher because of the cost of care for the uninsured.

We pay $15 billion more in taxes because of the cost of care for the uninsured. And it's trapped us in a vicious cycle. As the uninsured cause premiums to rise, more employers drop coverage. As more employers drop coverage, more people become uninsured, and premiums rise even further.

But the skeptics tell us that reform is too costly, too risky, too impossible for America.

Obsolete Technology

Well the skeptics must be living somewhere else. Because when you see what the health care crisis is doing to our families, to our economy, to our country, you realize that caution is what's costly. Inaction is what's risky. Doing nothing is what's impossible when it comes to health care in America.

It's time to act. This isn't a problem of money, this is a problem of will. A failure of leadership. We already spend $2.2 trillion a year on health care in this country. My colleague, Senator Ron Wyden, who's recently developed a bold new health care plan of his own, tells it this way:

Alternatives to the Current U.S. Health Care System

We could use prices to ration health services, for example, by requiring 50 percent co-payments; that would force people to receive less care, but not necessarily based on medical need. Perhaps we spend 14 percent of GDP [gross domestic product] on health care because that's how much we value it. If so, the best answer may lie not in reducing demand but in increasing supply. We could try federal and state deregulation and subsidies to sharply increase the numbers of doctors, nurses, and clinics over the next decade; and shorter patent protection periods could mean more generic-drug substitutes and cheaper versions of high-tech equipment. Maybe it would mean lower-quality care and fewer new drugs and technologies—but maybe not. And if it did slow health-care inflation, we might be able to get to universal coverage without breaking the budget or the bank.

Robert Shapiro, Slate.com, May 15, 2003. www.slate.com.

For the money Americans spent on health care last year, we could have hired a group of skilled physicians, paid each one of them $200,000 to care for just seven families, and guaranteed every single American quality, affordable health care.

So where's all that money going? We know that a quarter of it—one out of every four health care dollars—is spent on non-medical costs; mostly bills and paperwork. And we also know that this is completely unnecessary. Almost every other industry in the world has saved billions on these administrative costs by doing it all online. Every transaction you make at a bank now costs them less than a penny. Even at the Veterans

Administration, where it used to cost nine dollars to pull up your medical record, new technology means you can call up the same record on the internet for next to nothing.

But because we haven't updated technology in the rest of the health care industry, a single transaction still costs up to twenty-five dollars—not one dime of which goes toward improving the quality of our health care.

This is simply inexcusable, and if we brought our entire health care system online, something everyone from [Democratic Senator] Ted Kennedy to [Republican Representative] Newt Gingrich believes we should do, we'd already be saving over $600 million a year on health care costs.

The federal government should be leading the way here. If you do business with the federal employee health benefits program, you should move to an electronic claims system. If you are a provider who works with Medicare, you should have to report your patient's health outcomes, so that we can figure out, on a national level, how to improve health care quality. These are all things experts tell us must be done but aren't being done. And the federal government should lead.

Funding Drug Companies and the Health Care Industry

Another, more controversial area we need to look at is how much of our health care spending is going toward the record-breaking profits earned by the drug and health care industry. It's perfectly understandable for a corporation to try and make a profit, but when those profits are soaring higher and higher each year while millions lose their coverage and premiums skyrocket, we have a responsibility to ask why.

At a time when businesses are facing increased competition and workers rarely stay with one company throughout their lives, we also have to ask if the employer-based system of health care itself is still the best for providing insurance to all Americans. We have to ask what we can do to provide more

Americans with preventative care, which would mean fewer doctor's visits and less cost down the road. We should make sure that every single child who's eligible is signed up for the children's health insurance program, and the federal government should make sure that our states have the money to make that happen. And we have to start looking at some of the interesting ideas on comprehensive reform that are coming out of states like Maine and Illinois and California, to see what we can replicate on a national scale and what will move us toward that goal of universal coverage for all.

But regardless of what combination of policies and proposals get us to this goal, we must reach it. We must act. And we must act boldly. . . .

Action Has Produced Results

Half a century ago, America found itself in the midst of another health care crisis. For millions of elderly Americans, the single greatest cause of poverty and hardship was the crippling cost of health care and the lack of affordable insurance. Two out of every three elderly Americans had annual incomes of less than $1,000, and only one in eight had health insurance.

As health care and hospital costs continued to rise, more and more private insurers simply refused to insure our elderly, believing they were too great of a risk to care for.

The resistance to action was fierce. Proponents of health care reform were opposed by well-financed, well-connected interest groups who spared no expense in telling the American people that these efforts were "dangerous" and "un-American," "revolutionary" and even "deadly."

And yet the reformers marched on. They testified before Congress and they took their case to the country and they introduced dozens of different proposals but always, always they stood firm on their goal to provide health care for every American senior. And finally, after years of advocacy and negotiation and plenty of setbacks, President Lyndon Johnson signed the Medicare bill into law on July 30th of 1965.

The signing ceremony was held in Missouri, in a town called Independence, with the first man who was bold enough to issue the call for universal health care—President Harry Truman.

And as he stood with Truman by his side and signed what would become the most successful government program in history—a program that had seemed impossible for so long—President Johnson looked out at the crowd and said, "History shapes men, but it is a necessary faith of leadership that men can help shape history."

Never forget that we have it within our power to shape history in this country. It is not in our character to sit idly by as victims of fate or circumstance, for we are a people of action and innovation, forever pushing the boundaries of what's possible.

Now is the time to push those boundaries once more. We have come so far in the debate on health care in this country, but now we must finally answer the call first issued by Truman, advanced by Johnson, and fought for by so many leaders and Americans throughout the last century. The time has come for universal health care in America.

> *"Despite overwhelming evidence that single-payer health care systems do not provide high-quality care to all citizens regardless of ability to pay, proponents of socialized medicine tout such systems as models for the United States to emulate."*

The United States Does Not Need Universal Health Care

John C. Goodman

John C. Goodman states in the following viewpoint that, based on studies of European models of single-payer health care, universal health care is not the model the United States should adopt. Goodman debunks twelve myths of national health care, such as patients in countries with national health care have a right to care, or that they receive higher-quality care. Goodman believes that a market-driven health care system would be a better alternative to universal health care. John C. Goodman is president of the National Center for Policy Analysis in Dallas Texas.

John C. Goodman, "Health Care in a Free Society: Rebutting the Myths of National Health Insurance," Cato Institute, policy analysis no. 532, January 27, 2005. http://www.cato.org/pub_display.php?pub_id=3627.

As you read, consider the following questions:

1. According to Goodman, who is likely to get favored treatment if the government was put in charge of health care?

2. What is a good measure of a country's health care system, according to Goodman? Why don't infant mortality rates and life expectancy matter?

3. What are some factors that contribute to the high cost of health care in countries with national health plans, according to this study? How is the health care system in the United States keeping costs down?

Despite overwhelming evidence that single-payer health care systems do not provide high-quality care to all citizens regardless of ability to pay, proponents of socialized medicine tout such systems as models for the United States to emulate. Ironically, over the course of the past decade almost every European country with a national health care system has introduced market-oriented reforms and turned to the private sector to reduce health costs and increase the value, availability, and effectiveness of treatments. In making such changes, more often than not those countries looked to the United States for guidance. . . .

In each of these countries, growing frustration with government health programs has led to a reexamination of the fundamental principles of health care delivery. Through bitter experience, many of the countries that once touted the benefits of government control have learned that the surest remedy for their countries' health care crises is not increasing government power, but increasing patient power instead.

In this paper, we examine 12 popular myths about national health insurance. We have chosen to focus primarily, though not exclusively, on the health care systems of English-speaking countries whose cultures are similar to our own. Britain, Canada, and New Zealand in particular are often pointed to by advocates of national health insurance as models for U.S. health care system reform. In amassing evidence of how these systems actually work, many of our sources are government publications or commentary and analysis by reporters and scholars who fully support the concept of socialized medicine.

Myth No. 1: In Countries with National Health Insurance Systems, People Have a Right to Health Care

In fact, no country with national health insurance has established a right to health care. Citizens of Canada, for example, have no right to any particular health care service. They have no right to an MRI scan. They have no right to heart surgery. They do not even have the right to a place in line. The 100th person waiting for heart surgery is not entitled to the 100th surgery. Other people can and do jump the queue.

One could even argue that Canadians have fewer rights to health services than their pets. While Canadian pet owners can purchase an MRI scan for their cat or dog, purchasing a scan for themselves is illegal (although more and more human patients are finding legal loopholes, as we shall see below).

Countries with national health insurance limit health care spending by limiting supply. They do so primarily by imposing global budgets on hospitals and area health authorities and skimping on high-tech equipment. The result is rationing by waiting.

In Britain, with a population of almost 60 million, government statistics show that more than 1 million are waiting to be admitted to hospitals at any one time. In Canada, with a population of more than 31 million, the independent Fraser Institute found that more than 876,584 are waiting for treatment of all types. And in New Zealand, with a population of about 3.6 million, almost 111,000 people are on waiting lists for surgery and other treatments.

Although there may be some waiting in any health care system, in these countries rationing by waiting is government policy. Patients may wait for months or even years for treatment. For example, Canadian patients waited an average of 8.3 weeks in 2003 from the time they were referred to a specialist until the actual consultation, and another 9.5 weeks before treatment, including surgery. Of the 90,000 people waiting for surgery or treatment in New Zealand in 1997, more than 20,000 were waiting for a period of more than two years. The London-based Adam Smith Institute estimates that the people currently on NHS waiting lists will collectively wait about one million years longer to receive treatment than doctors deem acceptable.

Among the patients waiting, many are waiting in pain. Others are risking their lives. Delays in Britain for colon cancer treatment are so long that 20 percent of the cases considered curable at time of diagnosis are incurable by the time of treatment. During one 12-month period in Ontario, Canada, 71 patients died waiting for coronary bypass surgery while 121 patients were removed from the list because they had become too sick to undergo surgery with a reasonable chance of survival.

Myth No. 2: Countries with National Health Insurance Systems Deliver High-Quality Health Care

In countries with national health insurance, governments often attempt to limit demand for medical services by having fewer physicians. Because there are fewer physicians, they must see larger numbers of patients for shorter periods of time. U.S. physicians see an average of 2,222 patients per year, but physicians in Canada and Britain see an average of 3,143 and 3,176, respectively. Family practitioners in Canada bear even higher patient loads—on the average, more than 6,000 per year. Thus it is not surprising that 30 percent of American patients spend more than 20 minutes with their doctor on a visit, compared to 20 percent in Canada and only 5 percent in Britain.

When Americans see their doctors, they're more likely to receive treatments with hightech equipment.... The rate of renal dialysis in the United States is almost double that of Canada and almost three times that of Britain. Britain was the codeveloper with the United States of kidney dialysis in the 1960s, yet Britain consistently has had one of the lowest dialysis rates in Europe....

Myth No. 3: Countries with National Health Insurance Make Health Care Available on the Basis of Need Rather Than Ability to Pay

"The United States alone treats health care as a commodity distributed according to the ability to pay, rather than as a social service to be distributed according to medical need," claims Physicians for Single-Payer National Health Insurance. The idea that national health insurance makes health care available on the basis of need rather than ability to pay is an article of faith among supporters of socialized medicine.

But is it really true that national health insurance systems make care available on the basis of need alone? Precisely because of rationing, inefficiencies, and quality problems, patients in countries with national health insurance often spend their own money on health care when they are given an opportunity to do so. In fact, private-sector health care is the fastest-growing part of the health care system in many of these countries. For example, in Britain, 13 percent of the population has private health insurance to cover services to which they presumably are entitled for free under the NHS, and private-sector spending makes up 15 percent of the country's total health care spending.

In Canada, the share of privately funded health care spending rose from 24 percent in 1983 to an estimated 30.3 percent in 1998. In Australia, private health insurance coverage has risen from around 31 percent of the population in 1998 to almost 45 percent by March 2002. In New Zealand, 35 percent of the population has private health insurance (again, to cover services theoretically provided for free by the state), and private sector spending is about 10 percent of total health care spending. . . .

Myth No. 4: Although the United States Spends More per Capita on Health Care Than Countries with National Health Insurance, Americans Do Not Get Better Health Care

This myth is often supported by reference to two facts: (1) that life expectancy is not much different among the developed countries and (2) that the U.S. infant mortality rate is one of the highest among developed countries. If the United States spends more than other countries, why don't we rate higher than the others by these indices of health outcomes? The answer is that neither statistic is a good indicator of the quality of a country's health care system. Other indicators are much more telling.

Average life expectancy tells us almost nothing about the efficacy of health care systems because, throughout the developed world, there is very little correlation between health care spending and life expectancy. While a good health care system may, by intervention, extend the life of a small percentage of a population, it has very little to do with the average life span of the whole population. Instead, the number of years a person will live is primarily a result of genetic and social factors, including lifestyle, environment, and education. . . .

These factors have nothing to do with the quality of (or access to) health care.

A better measure of a country's health care system is mortality rates for those diseases that modern medicine can treat effectively. Take cancer, for example. In New Zealand and the United Kingdom nearly half of all women diagnosed with breast cancer die of the disease. In Germany and France, almost one in three dies of the disease. By contrast, in the United States only one in four women diagnosed with breast cancer dies of the disease. This is among the lowest rates of any industrial country. . . .

Myth No. 5: Countries with National Health Insurance Create Equal Access to Health Care

One of the most surprising features of national health insurance systems is the enormous amount of rhetoric devoted to the notion of equality and the importance of achieving it—especially in relation to the tiny amount of progress that appears to have been made. Aneurin Bevan, father of the NHS, declared that "everyone should be treated alike in the matter of medical care." But more than 30 years into the program (in the 1980s), an official task force (the Black Report) found little evidence that access to health care was any more equal than when the NHS was started. Almost 20 years later, a second task force (the Acheson Report) found evidence that access had become *less equal* in the years between the two studies. Across a range of indices, NHS performance figures have consistently shown widening gaps between the bestperforming and worst-performing hospitals and health authorities, as well as vastly different survival rates for different types of illness, depending on where patients live. The problem of unequal access is so well known in Britain that the press refers to the NHS as a "postcode lottery" in which a person's chances for timely, high-quality treatment depend on the neighborhood or "postcode" in which he or she lives.

Canadian officials also put a high premium on equality of access to medical care. In 1999, for instance, Health Minister Allan Rock stated that "equal access regardless of financial means will continue to be a cornerstone of our system." How well have the Canadians done? A series of studies from the University of British Columbia in the 1990s consistently found widespread inequality in the provision of care among British Columbia's 20 or so health regions. These studies are unique because researchers identified patients by the region in which they lived rather than the region where they received care. This allowed investigators to identify inequities in the amount of care received by residents of each region, including those patients forced to travel hundreds of miles (from one region to another) for treatment. . . .

Myth No. 6: Countries with National Health Insurance Hold Down Costs by Operating More Efficient Health Care Systems

A widely used measure of hospital efficiency is average length of stay (LOS). By this standard, U.S. hospitals are ahead of their international counterparts. The average length of a hospital stay in the United States is 5.4 days compared to 6.2 days in Australia, 9.0 in the Netherlands, and 9.6 in Germany. Whereas patients from other countries routinely convalesce in a hospital, American patients are more likely to recover at home.

It is an inefficient use of resources to fill an acute care hospital bed with a patient waiting for nonemergency care, a geriatric patient waiting to transfer to a nonacute facility, or simply because the hospital has not gotten around to discharging that patient. This is especially true when there are lengthy waiting lists for hospital admission. Generally, the more efficient the hospital, the more quickly it will admit and discharge patients.

Long-term care patients who should be in nursing homes, in geriatric wards, or at home are often found occupying acute care beds in Britain—a practice known as "bed blocking." As a result, many patients must wait for admission and treatment because patients treated earlier are waiting for discharge to an appropriate facility and thus "blocking" access to a bed. Officials estimate that about 3.3 percent of beds are blocked at any given time. Many public health officials think the actual number may be far higher. Liam Fox, admittedly the British Conservative Party's shadow health secretary and thus a Labor government critic, has estimated that the true number of blocked beds is closer to 15 percent.

The statistics on bed utilization indicate bed management in Britain is highly inefficient. More than one million people are waiting for medical treatment in British hospitals at any one time, and an estimated 500,000 surgeries were cancelled in the past five years because of the shortage of NHS hospital beds. Yet close to 30,000 beds (16 percent of the total) are empty on any given day. These estimates imply that as many as one out of three NHS hospital beds is unavailable for acute care patients.

A *British Medical Journal* comparison of the British NHS and Kaiser Permanente, a large U.S. health maintenance organization (HMO), concluded that the per capita costs of the two systems were similar. However, the analysis found that Kaiser provided its members with more comprehensive and convenient primary care services and much more rapid access to specialists and hospital admissions. After adjustments for differences between countries, the NHS cost was calculated at $1,764 per capita compared to a Kaiser cost of $1,951. However, Kaiser had two and one half times as many pediatricians, twice as many obstetricians-gynecologists, and three times as many cardiologists per enrollee as the NHS. After referral, waiting times to see a specialist were more than six times as long in the NHS. For nonemergency hospital admission, 90

percent of Kaiser patients waited less than three months; one-third of NHS patients waited more than five months.

One of the most striking differences between the two health systems was the length of stay. Kaiser had 270 acute care bed days per 1,000 population, whereas NHS patients stayed in the hospital more than three times as long—an average of 1,000 acute care bed days per 1,000 population. . . .

Myth No. 7: National Health Insurance Would Benefit the Elderly and Racial Minorities

It is frequently argued that national health insurance would benefit the elderly and reduce racial health disparities that exist in the United States. Empirical studies show this not to be the case. Minorities are often discriminated against under national health insurance. In a market where prices are used to allocate resources, goods and services are rationed by price. Willingness to pay determines which individuals utilize resources. In a nonmarket system, things are very different. Unable to discriminate on the basis of price, suppliers of services must discriminate among potential customers on the basis of other factors. Race and ethnic background are invariably among those factors.

In a recent study of Canadian India groups sampled had much less access to health care than Caucasians—despite their greater health needs. Futher, health disparities persisted between Canadian Indians and Caucasians. The infant death rate during the study period was 13.8 per 1,000 live births for Indian infants and 16.3 per 1,000 for Inuit infants, approximately twice the rate (7.3 per 1,000) of that for all Canadian infants during the same period. Overall, Canadian aboriginal people "die earlier than their fellow Canadians and sustain a disproportionate share of the burden of physical disease and mental illness.". . .

If the experience of other countries is any guide, the elderly have the most to lose under a national health insurance system. In general, when health care is rationed, the young get preferential treatment, while older patients get pushed to the rear of the waiting lines. . . .

Myth No. 8: Countries with National Health Insurance Systems Have Been More Successful Than the United States in Controlling Health Care Costs

The United States spends more on health care than any other country in the world, both in dollars per person and as a percentage of GDP [Gross Domestic Product]. Does that mean that our predominantly private health care system is less able to control spending than developed countries with national health insurance? Not necessarily.

Almost without exception, international comparisons show that wealthier countries spend a larger proportion of their GDP on health care. In his classic 1977 and 1981 studies, health economist Joseph Newhouse found that 90 percent of the variation in health care spending among developed countries is based on income alone.

Most international statistics on health care spending are produced by the Organization for Economic Cooperation and Development. However, OECD statistics are not always useful because different countries use different methods to report costs. No effective international guidelines exist, and some countries include services that others do not. For instance, the OECD definition of health care expenditures includes nursing home care. But while Germany includes nursing home care as part of total health expenditures, Britain does not. Some countries count hospital beds simply by counting metal frames with mattresses, whether or not they are in use. In others, a "bed" is counted only if it is staffed and operational. . . .

Not all health care prices are rising. Although health care inflation is robust for those services paid by third-party insurance, prices are rising only moderately for services patients buy directly. The real (inflation-adjusted) price of cosmetic surgery fell over the past decade—despite a huge increase in demand and considerable innovation. Cosmetic surgery is one of the few types of medical care for which consumers pay almost exclusively out of pocket. Even so, the demand for cosmetic surgery exploded in recent years. Despite the quadrupling of the number of surgeries, cosmetic surgeons' fees remained relatively stable.

Myth No. 9: Single-Payer National Health Insurance Would Reduce the Cost of Prescription Drugs for Americans

Advocates of single-payer insurance maintain that it would provide all Americans with full coverage for necessary drugs and control drug costs by establishing a national formulary—a list of drugs available to patients under the national heath plan—and negotiating drug prices with manufacturers "based on their costs (excluding marketing and lobbying)." However, access to new, more effective (and more expensive) prescription drugs is often restricted in countries with national health insurance.

Drug development is costly. Only one in five drugs tested ever reaches the public, and the cost of bringing a new drug to market now averages $900 million. A government facing rising health care costs is tempted to negotiate prices just above the costs of production, ignoring the research and development (R&D) costs. Countries with single-payer systems thus reap the benefits of new drugs without sharing the burden of their development. As a result, many pharmaceutical firms based in single-payer countries have gone abroad to recoup their costs, and drug innovation is limited. . . .

Trust in Inventiveness and Free Markets

The market, which is nothing more than individuals acting purposively to achieve desired ends, has delivered solutions to the problems of human existence that have raised civilization to the heights we now enjoy. Few seem to appreciate the creative nature of free markets.

The same creative market forces that have improved life immeasurably over the thousands of years of human existence would surely work out a system better than political-minded bureaucrats in Washington would. The problem with the health care debate is that somehow the government has become the central agent of change and leadership, instead of the creative forces of freethinking individuals. The most unfortunate thing is that this problem is not confined to the health care industry, but that it permeates the political thinking of American life in all of its facets.

Christopher Mayer, "Health Care for All,"
Ludwig von Mises Institute, June 10, 2003. www.mises.org.

Myth No. 10: Under National Health Insurance, Funds Are Allocated So That They Have the Greatest Impact on Health

The one characteristic of foreign health care systems that strikes American observers as the most bizarre is the way in which limited resources are allocated. Foreign governments do not merely deny lifesaving medical technology to patients under national insurance schemes. They also take money that could be spent saving lives and curing disease and spend it serving people who are not seriously ill. Often, the spending has little if anything to do with health care.

The British National Health Service's emphasis on "caring" rather than "curing" marks a radical difference between British and American health care. The tendency throughout the NHS is to divert funds from expensive care for the small number who are seriously ill toward the large number who seek relatively inexpensive services for minor ills. Take British ambulance service, for example. British "patients" take between 18 million and 19 million ambulance rides each year—about one ride for every three people in Britain. Almost 80 percent of these rides are for such nonemergency purposes as taking an outpatient to a hospital or a senior to a pharmacy and amount to little more than free taxi service. While thousands of people die each year from lack of kidney dialysis, the NHS provides an array of comforts for chronically ill people with less serious health problems. For example, the NHS provides nonmedical services to about 1.5 million people a year. These include day care services to more than 260,000, home care or home help services to 578,000, home alterations for 375,000, and occupational therapy for 300,000. . . .

Myth No. 11: A Single-Payer National Health Care System Would Lower Health Care Costs Because Preventive Health Services Would Be More Widely Available

Proponents of national health insurance often argue that because care is "free" at the point of service, people will be more likely to seek preventive services. Thus, money will be saved when doctors catch conditions in their early stages before they develop into expensive-to-treat diseases. Yet the evidence shows that patients in government-run health care systems do not get more preventive care than Americans do, and even if they did, such care would not save the government money.

Preventive care may even be less available under a single-payer system *because* care is free. A comparison of American and British physicians in the 1990s found that the British saw a physician almost as often as Americans (roughly six times a year). Yet when Americans did see a doctor, the consultation was six times as likely to last more than 20 minutes. A recent survey of 200 British GPs and more than 2,000 consumers found that 87 percent of smokers want more advice and help in quitting from their GPs, but 93 percent of GPs say they lack the time to give such advice. Moreover, British physicians have much less access to diagnostic equipment and must send their patients to hospitals for chest X-rays and simple blood tests. In Canada, fee structures are designed to discourage physicians from providing office-based procedures. Doctors can only bill for the time they spend examining and evaluating patients, not for diagnostic tests. Access to preventive care—which is often costly in itself—is tacitly discouraged by cash-strapped health care bureaucracies.

If anything, the amount of preventive care people get under single-payer systems seems to be based more on socioeconomic status and education than on whether medical care is "free" or not. Studies comparing women in Ontario and in two areas of the United States found that their chances of receiving a Pap smear or clinical breast cancer screening increased with education and income regardless of whether a woman had health insurance.

Myth No. 12: The Defects of National Health Insurance Schemes in Other Countries Could Be Remedied by a Few Reforms

The characteristics described above are not accidental byproducts of government-run health care systems. They are the natural and inevitable consequences of placing the market for health care under the control of politicians. Health care delivery in countries with national health insurance does not just happen to be as it is. In many respects, it could not be otherwise.

Why are low-income patients so frequently discriminated against under national health insurance? Because such insurance is almost always a middle-class phenomenon. Prior to its introduction, every country had some government-funded program to meet the health care needs of the poor. The middle-class working population not only paid for its own health care but also paid taxes to fund health care for the poor. National health insurance extends the "free ride" to those who pay taxes to support it. Such systems respond to the political demands of the middle-class population, and they serve the interests of this population.

Why do national health insurance schemes skimp on expensive services to the seriously ill while providing so many inexpensive services to ter services benefit millions of people (read: millions of voters), while acute and intensive care services concentrate large amounts of money on a handful of patients (read: small numbers of voters). Democratic political pressures in this case dictate the redistribution of resources from the few to the many.

Why are sensitive rationing decisions and other issues of hospital management left to hospital bureaucracies? Because the alternative—to have those decisions made by politicians—is politically impossible. As a practical matter, no government can make it a national policy to let 25,000 of its citizens die from lack of the best cancer treatment every year. Nor can any government announce that some people must wait for surgery so that the elderly can use hospitals as nursing homes, or that elderly patients must be moved so that surgery can proceed. These decisions are so emotionally loaded that no elected official could afford to claim responsibility for them. Important decisions on who will receive care and how that care will be delivered are left to the hospital bureaucracy because no other course is politically possible.

Why do the rich and the powerful manage to jump the queues and obtain care that is denied to others? Because they are the people with the power to change the system. If they had to wait in line for their care like ordinary people, the system would not last for a minute. . . .

Conclusion

The realities of national health insurance documented in this paper—waiting lines, rationing, lack of cutting-edge medical technology, restricted access to the latest prescription drugs, inequitable distribution of care—are not accidental. Such problems flow inexorably from the fact that politicians and bureaucrats—not patients and doctors—are given the authority to allocate limited health care resources. . . .

"Uninsured Americans cannot always see a doctor when they need to, and they do not get the care they should."

Too Many Americans Lack Health Insurance

Risa Lavizzo-Mourey

Risa Lavizzo-Mourey is the president and CEO of the Robert Wood Johnson Foundation, a fundraising institution that seeks to improve health care in America. In the following viewpoint, Lavizzo-Mourey states that the United States has too many uninsured individuals and families. She blames this in part on the failing economy because health insurance coverage is typically tied to employment. Lavizzo-Mourey argues that the lack of insurance has forced many people to forego treatment and has exacerbated the consequences associated with routine preventative illnesses. She insists that some remedy must be found, for the lack of health insurance is jeopardizing the welfare of the nation.

As you read, consider the following questions:

1. According to Lavizzo-Mourey, what percentage of America's children do not receive health insurance coverage?

Risa Lavizzo-Mourey, "Critical Condition: 6.6 Million Uninsured in Nation's Largest State," *San Francisco Chronicle*, May 1, 2005, p. C1. Reproduced by permission of the author.

2. As the author reports, what percentage of uninsured adults report not having a personal physician or health care provider?

3. What is the main thing America is missing in terms of solving the problem of the uninsured?

[P resident] Ronald Reagan used to say that "status quo" is Latin for "the mess that we're in." Well, for too many working Americans and their families, the health care status quo is a real mess.

What makes it such a mess? More than 45 million Americans (6.6 million Californians, including 779,000 children) do not have health insurance. These men, women, and children make up nearly 16 percent of our population.

Who are the uninsured? Eight in 10 are in working families with modest incomes. More than 1 in 10 children go without coverage. Why? Their parents earn too much to be enrolled in public programs. Yet these working moms and dads do not earn enough to buy private coverage for their kids.

When many low- and middle-income Americans lose their jobs, they lose their health insurance, which they find it nearly impossible to replace on their own. They can't afford to pay $10,000 a year, the average price for a family policy for four.

It is by economics that we ration care today. We do it by pricing out working Americans who are neither prosperous nor impoverished. This is a true mess, and it is simply unacceptable.

Not being able to afford insurance has serious health consequences. Uninsured Americans cannot always see a doctor when they need to, and they do not get the care they should.

Problems of the Uninsured

A report released [in April 2005] analyzing data from the federal Centers for Disease Control and Prevention found that at least 20 million working Americans do not have medical insurance of any kind.

These uninsured adults are going without needed medical care—41 percent of uninsured adults report being unable to see a doctor when needed in the past 12 months because of cost. Only 9 percent who have coverage found themselves in that bind.

In addition, 56 percent of uninsured adults without health insurance say they do not have a personal doctor or health care provider, compared with just 16 percent of people with coverage. The problem is pervasive in every state.

Without proper preventive care, adults with chronic conditions are less likely to get the routine care that keeps them active, productive, even alive. According to the Institute of Medicine, people without health insurance are four times more likely to experience an avoidable hospital or emergency room visit. Even worse, an estimated 18,000 Americans die prematurely each year because they don't have health insurance.

This isn't surprising when you consider, as the *New England Journal of Medicine* reported, that uninsured women with breast cancer have a 30 to 50 percent higher risk of dying than do women with private coverage. According to the *Journal of National Cancer Institute*, uninsured patients with colorectal cancer are about 50 percent more likely to die than patients with private coverage, even when the cancer is diagnosed at similar stages.

Sticking to the Status Quo

We know the status quo is a mess, but what do we do about it?

Many of us have our fix, the choice we prefer over all others: tax credits, public programs, business mandates, individual mandates, association health plans, a combination of some or all of these options, or a completely public program like Canada's.

2006 Health Insurance Coverage Statistics

• Both the percentage and the number of people without health insurance increased in 2006. The percentage without health insurance increased from 15.3 percent in 2005 to 15.8 percent in 2006 and the number of uninsured increased from 44.8 million to 47.0 million.

• The number of people with health insurance increased to 249.8 million in 2006 (up from 249.0 million in 2005). In 2006, the number of people covered by private health insurance (201.7 million) and the number of people covered by government health insurance (80.3 million) were not statistically different from 2005.

• The percentage of people covered by employment-based health insurance decreased to 59.7 percent in 2006 from 60.2 percent in 2005.

• The percentage of people covered by government health programs decreased to 27.0 percent in 2006 from 27.3 percent in 2005. The percentage and the number of people covered by Medicaid were statistically unchanged at 12.9 percent and 38.3 million, respectively, in 2006.

• The percentage and the number of children under 18 years old without health insurance increased to 11.7 percent and 8.7 million in 2006 (from 10.9 percent and 8.0 million, respectively, in 2005). With an uninsured rate in 2006 at 19.3 percent, children in poverty were more likely to be uninsured than all children.

• The uninsured rate and the number of uninsured in 2006 were not statistically different from 2005 for non-Hispanic Whites (at 10.8 percent and 21.2 million). The percentage and the number of uninsured Blacks increased (from 19.0 percent and 7.0 million in 2005) to 20.5 percent and 7.6 million in 2006 (Table 6).

• The percentage and the number of uninsured Hispanics increased to 34.1 percent and 15.3 million in 2006.

U.S. Census Bureau, 2006. www.census.gov.

But every time we get serious about changing the status quo, too many of us stick to our own fix and refuse to budge. The only consensus we reach is that the status quo—the mess we are in—is the least objectionable choice to the most people.

This may sound idealistic, even naive, but something has to give. The mess must be solved. Health care is not a policy, product or political gotcha—it is something everyone needs.

There is no responsible reason for not acting. The main thing we are missing is leadership.

Accepting the status quo isn't an alternative. The number of uninsured Americans is too large. The number of people at risk of losing their coverage is too great. The consequences of inaction for everyone are too serious.

"We should celebrate every time Americans free themselves from unnecessary and oppressively overpriced government-mandated health insurance."

Americans Do Not Need Health Insurance

Carla Howell

Carla Howell heads the Center For Small Government and is the publisher of Small Government News, *an online e-mail newsletter advocating the end of intrusive, controlling, and expansive government. In the following viewpoint, Howell argues that health insurance is a waste of money. She contends patients and providers have no incentive to keep costs under control, and therefore prices continue to rise even as care does not improve. Howell believes that most people have enough savings or access to credit to pay for health emergencies when needed and are thus surrendering large portions of their wages every month to fund unused care. She maintains that because "big government" is mandating and subsidizing health care, it is behind the high costs and the current drain on people's incomes.*

As you read, consider the following questions:

1. In Howell's view, what are above-average wage earners better off putting their money into rather than spending it on health care?
2. Why can excessive treatment put one's health at risk, according to Howell?
3. Why is "big government" responsible for high health care costs, in the author's opinion?

Socialized medicine's true believers—who dominate the ranks of mainstream news reporters and politicians—try to bludgeon us into believing that the lack of medical insurance is a crisis, a disaster, and a never-ending emergency.

Here's an example of how a news report typically casts the "uninsured":

> "The number of uninsured or underinsured people in the United States is estimated to be about 46 million. . . they sit on the edge of catastrophe." (*Journal Times*, Wisconsin, February 27, 2006)

But "uninsured" Americans are usually nowhere near "catastrophe." They have plenty of access to urgent care when they need it.

Moreover, they save themselves a boatload of money by steering clear of one of America's biggest money pits: health insurance.

We don't need more insurance in America. We need much less.

The Black Hole of Medical Insurance

Americans who don't have health insurance are often neither poor nor do they lack access to medical care. They simply choose not to buy insurance because they believe it's a bad use of their money.

In Massachusetts—the Overpriced Health Care Capital of the World—young, healthy families can spend over $9,400 a year for the cheapest HMO policy they can find, and over $19,800 for a broader coverage plan. Families with middle-aged parents can spend over $30,000—every year—to be insured. The older you are, the more unaffordable it gets.

What's worse, these exorbitant prices don't even guarantee that you'll be covered. A policy's fine print gives insurance companies the option to terminate your coverage if your care drags on too long. The insured who suffer from a serious disease or medical trauma have to turn to the same government welfare programs they would if they had no insurance at all. What's the point of buying an insurance policy that doesn't insure you in your times of greatest need?

The "Uninsured" Are Smart Investors

The "uninsured" are portrayed as poor, desolate souls on the brink of "catastrophe." But contrary to media propaganda, they have access to the health care they need.

The wealthy don't need health insurance. Their money is better spent on investments that provide a return. They can easily cover the cost of treating a serious medical condition.

Many above-average wage earners don't need insurance either. They're better off investing their money in their retirement and withdrawing funds for health care only if there's a need.

Even people with no cash savings to fall back on—average and below-average income families—are often able to insure themselves. They may have an IRA or equity in a home or business they can borrow against in the event of an emergency. Although a serious illness could wipe out their assets, they at least have a chance of building wealth—and not depleting what assets they have by forking over huge sums for an overpriced medical insurance policy.

Individuals and families that invest the money they would otherwise spend on medical insurance can build a nest egg worth over $100,000 in just 5 years. In 10 years it could grow to over $250,000—enough to cover a major health care catastrophe. Or buy a house. If they continue to enjoy good health, they can retire as millionaires.

Hazards of Medical Insurance

There are other good reasons to avoid medical insurance.

Whenever an insurance company pays for health services, it drives up everyone's cost—yours included—and renders health care services clumsy, inefficient, and even dangerous.

Neither patients nor providers have incentive to keep costs down. This encourages doctors to prescribe procedures you don't need—raising costs for insurance companies. They respond in turn by raising the price of your premiums, raising the amount you must pay for co-pays and deductibles, and reducing the services they cover.

In addition, excess treatment can put your health at risk. Patients who undergo unnecessary tests, operations, and drug regimens sometimes end up with worse medical problems than they started with.

At the same time, insurance rules forbid practitioners from giving you services you actually need. Again, your health suffers.

When you pay directly for services, you or someone you trust is in the driver's seat. You and your health care providers have direct incentive to give you high-quality care at a reasonable price.

Medical insurance co-pays, deductibles, and coverage denials make medical bills confusing and hard to read. Billing errors are common—and difficult to correct. You're forced to either pay what your bill instructs you to pay or to try to avoid overpayment by submerging yourself in paperwork that can be as complicated and infuriating as filing taxes.

Impact of Rising Costs on Employers and Employees

- The annual premium that a health insurer charges an employer for a health plan covering a family of four averaged $11,500 in 2006. Workers contributed nearly $3,000, or 10 percent, more than they did in 2005. The annual premiums for family coverage significantly eclipsed the gross earnings for a full-time, minimum-wage worker ($10,712).

- Workers are now paying $1,094 more in premiums annually for family coverage than they did in 2000.

- Health insurance expenses are the fastest growing cost component for employers. Unless something changes dramatically, health insurance costs will overtake profits by 2008.

- The average employee contribution to company-provided health insurance has increased more than 143 percent since 2000. Average out-of-pocket costs for deductibles, co-payments for medications, and co-insurance for physician and hospital visits rose 115 percent during the same period.

National Coalition on Health Care, 2007. www.nchc.org.

The best way to minimize billing hassles is to forgo medical insurance and pay your providers directly for medical services.

Why the Insurance Scam Exists

Many Americans have insurance because Big Government mandates it, subsidizes it, and provides tax incentives for it.

Seniors are forced to sign up for Medicare, or they forfeit their Social Security checks. Taxpayers are forced to fund high-priced health plans for government employees. Employers are forced to provide their employees insurance.

If employers were free to use the tax-free money they now spend on medical insurance to pay tax-free wages instead, many employees would far prefer the higher wages. It's a much better deal.

Others buy insurance, or seek a job that provides insurance, because of the horror stories they've heard about how expensive medical bills can be. A catastrophic care episode can cost tens, even hundreds, of thousands of dollars and leave a family in dire financial straights.

Big Government is directly responsible for these high costs. Thousands of state and federal laws, regulations, mandates, and subsidies drive up the cost of health care. What should be a minimal part of the family budget is a backbreaking expense. If we end Big Government Health Care, prices will drop dramatically. Far fewer people will need or want insurance.

Rather than end these disastrous Big Government Health Care Programs and allow prices to drop, Big Government Politicians seek to expand them. They keep the demand for insurance artificially high.

People also seek insurance because Big Government outlaws health care charity, leaving poor people with medical problems nowhere else to turn but to Big Government welfare programs.

Years ago, medical special interests convinced politicians to shut down free clinics for the poor, once common in the United States. Rather than allow them to reopen, socialized medicine advocates claim that the high cost of health care is the fault of people who refuse to buy insurance and who run to a hospital emergency room instead every time they have a problem. What they never admit is that Big Government Politicians cut off poor people from life-saving, zero-cost, tax-free alternatives.

Bemoaning the "uninsured" is a ruse. Big Government Politicians drive up the cost of health care. They drive affordable free-market alternatives out of business. Then they blame the taxpayer for not buying health insurance—made unaffordable by Big Government. It's a scam.

Get Big Government out of Health Care

We must reject calls for more insurance. Rather, we should celebrate every time Americans free themselves from unnecessary and oppressively overpriced government-mandated health insurance.

What we need is to bring down the high cost of health care by removing Big Government health care prohibitions, mandates, regulations, and subsidies. We must vote against every politician who refuses to tear them down. Who deny us our health freedom.

When we separate health care from government, we'll dissolve the government-created demand for needless, high-priced medical insurance. We will enjoy higher quality, cost-conscious health care. We'll take $1 trillion every year from overpriced medical spending—and put it back in the pockets of working Americans.

Periodical Bibliography

The following articles have been selected to supplement the diverse views presented in this chapter.

Julie Appleby   "Universal Care Appeals to USA," *USA Today*, October 16, 2006.

Catherine Arnst   "The Doctor Will See You—In Three Months," *Business Week*, July 9, 2007.

Richard S. Dunham   "Stopping Reform Before It Starts," *Business* and Keith Epstein   *Week*, April 16, 2007.

Economist   "Creeps and Bounds," July 21, 2007.

John Edwards   "One for All," *Modern Healthcare*, July 23, 2007.

Thomas K. Grose   "Free Health Coverage for All," *U.S. News and World Report*, March 26, 2007.

Peter Harkness   "Prognosis Upgraded," *CQ Researcher*, May 21, 2007.

Phillip Longman   "The Best Care Anywhere," *Washington Monthly*, January/February 2005.

Patrick Range   "Health Care, and How to Fix It," *Advocate*, McDonald   August 28, 2007.

National Review   "Against Universal Coverage," July 9, 2007.
Online

New Republic   "Health of Nations," March 19, 2007.

New York Times   "World's Best Medical Care," August 12, 2007.

Ruy Teixeira   "Healthcare for All?" Mother Jones, September 27, 2005.

OPPOSING
VIEWPOINTS®
SERIES

CHAPTER 2

How Should National Health Care Be Restructured?

Chapter Preface

In 2003 President George W. Bush began promoting the use of Health Savings Accounts (HSAs) so that individuals could have another option to pay for medical expenses. HSAs are privately owned savings accounts funded by individuals and then tapped over time to pay for everything from doctor visits to health emergencies. These accounts—and employer-funded health reimbursement accounts (which are similar to HSAs)—are part of a relatively new scheme to emphasize consumer-driven health care. The concept of consumer-driven health care is to put individuals in control of how their money is spent on health care. As Greg Scandlen writes in the following chapter, "Whether the payer is the government, an insurance company, or an employer, every penny spent on health care comes from the consumer in the form of taxes, premiums, or earned compensation. Consumers may allow these payers to use the money as long as they believe there is value added by doing so." Or, as Scandlen notes, consumers may find their own way to spend their health care dollars and limit the need for third-party assistance.

Insurance companies—those third-party providers—are still part of the current health care equation. Even HSAs involve contracting with an insurance company to pay for catastrophic coverage in case of serious and protracted illness. Most insurance plans today fall under the category of managed care, in which the insurer acts as an overseer to control costs by selecting care based on price and performance, approving only necessary tests and treatments, and restricting patient care to a network of physicians, specialists, and hospitals. Roughly nine out of ten health plans in America involve some form of managed care. And unlike HSAs, managed care—as its name implies—affords consumers little or no control of health care spending.

Managed care was successful in keeping costs from rapidly escalating during part of the 1990s, but in the twenty-first century, prices have begun to rise again. Arnold S. Relman, the former editor of the *New England Journal of Medicine*, asserts that the increases are because managed care has already cut all the costs it can, while "new and more expensive technology continues to come on line, inexorably pushing up medical expenditures." Relman believes the managed care system will likely be unable to contain costs in the future. He acknowledges that the solution to the current crisis will either involve bringing competition into the managed care system or to adopting a single-payer scheme (such as universal health care) in which managed care organizations and all intermediary agents are eliminated and money goes directly to physicians, hospitals, and other health care providers. In the following chapter, various critics offer other views of how to restructure health care in America in light of managed care's apparent failure to contain costs.

| *"Consumer driven health plans are designed to address the major objectives of managed care, development of healthful behaviors and containment of health care costs."*

Consumer Driven Health Care Will Enhance the Health Care System

Ronald Lagoe, Deborah L. Aspling, and Gert P. Westert

In the following viewpoint, researchers find that consumer driven health care plans seem to be on the rise. The growing popularity of these plans as an alternative to managed care plans is explored. Ronald Lagoe PhD, is executive director of the Hospital Executive Council in Syracuse, New York. Deborah Aspling RN, MBA, is vice president/chief operating officer at Lodi Memorial Hospital in Lodi, California, and commander of the 349th Air Mobility Wing of the United States Air Force at Travis Air Force Base. Dr. Gert Westert is coordinator of Health Services Research, RIVM, The National Institute for Public Health and the Environment, Bilthoven, The Netherlands.

As you read, consider the following questions:

1. What forms has the increase in consumer involvement in health care in the United States taken?
2. What major objectives are consumer-driven health-care plans designed to address?
3. What arguments are made by opponents of consumer-driven health-care plans?

The Rise of Consumer-Driven Health Care

The decline of managed care as the major driver of health care policy and reimbursement within the United States has opened the way for new forces to shape this area. The nature of these forces became visible in the late 1990s as managed care plans shifted responsibility for health care decision making to consumers. The resulting annual increases in health care expenditure were also effectively shifted to consumers through higher premiums, deductibles, and copayments. For example, in preferred provider organizations, the most widely used health plans, single coverage deductibles increased more than 50 percent between 2002 and 2003. More employers began offering high deductible plans. The rate of increase of out of pocket spending has increased every year between 2000 and 2003.

The rise of increased consumer involvement in health care in the United States has developed on several fronts. At the broadest level, it has taken the form of a greater consumer role in decision making concerning treatment. In the late 1990's the use of television, newspapers, and electronic media to market health care to consumers became pervasive. Drug companies became major users of this approach. They have conducted enormous media campaigns to promote the use of sexual stimulants, allergy medicines, and cosmetic treatments. Access to large marketing budgets has made it possible for these companies to reach millions of consumers with their messages. Local and regional diagnostic firms have also marketed magnetic resonance imaging and whole body scanning through similar campaigns.

These efforts have been successful because they gone directly to users of health care. They have circumvented insurance companies, managed care, and even physicians. Listeners are urged to 'ask' or 'tell' their doctor to prescribe any number of medications or tests. The clear message of all of these initiatives is for individual consumers to take a greater role in health care decision making. Greater user involvement in health care that was stimulated by the decline of managed care, as well as media initiatives of the pharmaceutical industry and other groups, have led directly to the development of a new type of health insurance in the United States, the consumer driven health plan. These mechanisms complete the change initiated by the decline of managed care by directly assigning health care decision-making to consumers.

Components of Consumer-Driven Health Cares

Consumer driven health plans are designed to address the major objectives of managed care, development of healthful behaviors and containment of health care costs. Components of consumer driven plans usually include the following.

High deductibles as incentives for greater consumer participation in the cost of care

Catastrophic coverage for high cost services such as inpatient hospitalization

Consumer savings accounts for funding of prevention and screening services

Procedures for roll over of unused savings account balances to future time periods

Support for consumer decision making through availability of internet based information concerning health care risk factors and provider outcomes

Tracking of employee health expenses through the system.

How to Make Consumer-Driven Health Care Happen

Employer-based consumer-driven health care requires the following steps:

1. Offering a number of highly differentiated health insurance policies that vary in benefits, out-of-pocket payments, and term (i.e. length of the policy). These options should include ones in which providers can freely create and price their offerings.

2. Subsidizing each plan by the same dollar amount so that enrollees' costs follow those of the company. Currently, many employers subsidize different plans by different amounts so that the enrollee does not understand the company's underlying costs.

3. Offering excellent information about the clinical and patient satisfaction of the providers in each plan. Consumers are much more interested in data about the quality of providers than the quality of health plans, and providers can play a much larger role in reshaping health care costs than insurers.

4. Offering excellent education and support.

5. Getting out of the way.

These five rules will enable financial executives to tame the health care cost monster, not by "just saying no" to consumers and providers, but with an old-fashioned American market-based system that enables demand and supply to create better, cheaper health care.

Regina Herzlinger,
Journal of Financial Service Professionals,
March 2004.

These components have been designed to replace structures of managed care plans which addressed the same objectives. Encouragement of healthful behaviors and health status objectives are addressed through consumer savings accounts, rollover provisions, and internet based information. These provisions have effectively transferred responsibility for the management of care from the primary care physician gatekeepers employed by managed care plans to the consumer. This transfer has been supported by a combination of financial incentives and electronic data.

Cost Containment

Consumer driven health plans also contain provisions for cost containment. High deductibles and catastrophic coverage are intended to limit expenditures by payors. These provisions effectively reduce expenses for many of the pharmaceutical and ambulatory care expenses currently being pushed by media advertising. By excluding payor reimbursement for them, these plans are transferring these expenses to the consumers, or providing incentives to eliminate the purchases altogether. This amounts to a cost containment approach very different from the utilization controls employed by managed care plans.

The implementation of consumer driven health plans has generated extensive controversy in the American health care system. Supporters of this approach have argued that it is logical because it places major responsibility for health care decision making in the hands of the party who will be most influenced by those decisions, the consumer. They have emphasized that, under these plans, positive health care behaviors and decision making are rewarded by fewer out of pocket expenses. They have also noted that consumers are provided with extensive electronic information needed to support effective decision-making.

Supporters of consumer driven plans also have suggested that these approaches include realistic mechanisms for health care cost containment. They have pointed out that managed care relied on limitations on the utilization of care to limit spending, while consumer driven plans assign these decisions to users of care. They have suggested that the new approach can satisfy both the payor and the consumer, by limiting insurance expenses for care and allowing individuals to purchase additional service.

Opponents Favor Managed Care

Opponents of consumer driven health care have argued that this approach is inferior to managed care, that it is a mechanism for employers and payors to abdicate their responsibilities. They have suggested that, rather than supporting consumers with the advice of physicians and other health care providers, it turns them loose to make decisions on their own. They have indicated that a set of financial incentives and internet based information is no substitute for the relationship between a patient and a caregiver.

Opponents of consumer driven plans also argued that the real purpose of these approaches is financial, that they are better identified as defined contribution plans. Opponents of these plans suggested that they are really covers for the abdication of financial responsibility by payors. They have argued that the major purpose of these plans is to shift health care costs from employers to employees. They have contended that high deductibles and catastrophic coverage are the real solution for employers and payors seeking to reduce premiums, regardless of the impact on subscribers.

The debate concerning consumer driven health care is probably only beginning in the United States. It bears similarities to the discussion surrounding the rise of managed care in the 1970s and 80s. One important difference between these situations may be the economic background. The ascendancy of managed care developed against the background of an upturn. Consumer driven care is developing at a time of economic instability and limited resources. Indeed, these conditions may be supporting the rise of the new approach.

Consumer-Driven Plans Still Evolving

A review of the current status on consumer driven plans suggests that they are still evolving. Many of these plans are still developing their own provider networks. Others are partnering with existing plans in order to expedite the process. Some plans are developing generic fee schedules for services and allowing consumers to develop their own networks. Consistent with this approach, consumers cover additional health care costs from their own resources.

The development of information infrastructure has become an important part of the implementation of consumer driven plans. In order to involve consumers in a meaningful way, plans must make available extensive electronic data to support decision making. These data include a variety of online sources of information including many types of research. They also must include financial information concerning provider prices and discounts. In order to enable consumers to participate in health care decision making on a continuing basis, plans must also make available data concerning consumer accounts which identify the impact of choices on available funds. The plans which are entering the consumer driven market in a serious manner must have all of these information resources available. They require an extensive investment in data infrastructure.

The implementation of consumer driven health plans is proceeding rapidly in the United States. Because of the size of the American population, it still occupies a relatively small proportion of the health care market. By 2004 enrollment in consumer driven health plans is projected to reach 1,000,000. This enrollment is still dwarfed by existing traditional insurance and managed care populations.

The future of consumer driven health care in the United States is difficult to predict. Additional time and utilization data will be required to determine whether this approach generates sufficient enrollment to develop into a major force within the health care system of the United States and whether other nations adopt it.

> *"How can a citizen be expected to know what health care services to buy and what not to buy if they don't have a medical degree?"*

Consumer-Driven Health Care May Exacerbate the Health Care Crisis

Gail Shearer

In the following viewpoint Gail Shearer, the director of Health Policy Analysis at the Consumer's Union, contends that high-deductible consumer-driven health plans may fail to serve people with chronic illnesses or parents of children with such conditions because of the constant drain on personal finances.

As you read, consider the following questions:

1. What is "driving" high-deductible health plans, according to Shearer?

2. As Shearer states, what percentage of American families incurred out-of-pocket expenses that exceeded 10 percent of their annual income?

Gail Shearer, Testimony before the Joint Economic Committee on Impact of "Consumer-Driven" Health Care on Consumers, Yonkers, NY: 2004. Copyright © 2004 by the Consumers Union of U.S., Yonkers, NY 10703-1057, A non-profit organization. Reproduced by permission.

3. What are some of the pitfalls consumers will experience with high-deductable plans, according to Shearer?

Defining features of so-called "consumer-driven health care" plans tend to be high-deductible policies (e.g., $5,000), combined with a contribution by the employer to a health care savings account, at a level that leaves the consumer exposed to some out-of-pocket costs before the high deductible is met. For example, the employer might provide $2,000 toward a family's health reimbursement account, and offer a deductible of $5,000. (Often, the employer provides additional access to information about health care choices, such as information about managing certain diseases.) "Consumer-driven" implies that consumers have a full range of choices, and are in the driver's seat calling the shots. The problem with this is that too many consumers are not in control of their health care out-of-pocket costs or health coverage. An employee with a seriously, chronically ill child, for example, will not be able to accumulate a nest egg in a health reimbursement account, and will face high out-of-pocket costs each year. A consumer with an income in the range of $25,000 to $30,000 will suffer financial hardship if they face out-of-pocket costs as high as $3,000 a year. An employee with existing health conditions such as high blood pressure or diabetes will face very limited choices in the individual marketplace if his employer decides to "cash out" its health insurance plan and send employees into the individual market for coverage. This type of policy appears to be driven largely by the employer's desire to curb its health care expenditures. The term "consumer-driven" may well mislead employees and the public about the true impact of this type of coverage. . . .

The Risks of Being Underinsured

[In 2002], approximately one in six (16 percent) families (with head of household under 65) incurred out-of-pocket health care costs (including premiums they pay directly) that exceed

---

Managing Paperwork as Well as Health Care Decisions

With a high-deductible policy, expect to get the provider's bills, explanation-of-benefit forms and a blizzard of other paperwork, all of which you'll be responsible for directly.

And if you open a tax-advantaged savings account— these are often offered with high-deductible policies—be sure to save your receipts and cultivate your record-keeping skills. Depending on the account, you may have employer contributions mingling with your own contributions. . . .

By comparison, managed care plan enrollees usually don't see provider bills, and only pay co-payments and premiums, typically deducted straight from their paychecks.

Christopher J. Gearon, Washington Post, *October 18, 2005.*

---

10 percent of their income. Economists have used a risk-based definition of the underinsured—in which individuals are "underinsured" if they have private insurance and yet, because it is not comprehensive, run the risk of having out-of-pocket costs exceeding 10 percent of their income if they face a catastrophic illness. . . . High-deductible (and "consumer-driven") health care plans are designed to increase out-of-pocket costs for those who have health care expenditures. The gap between money in a health savings account and the high-deductible (this gap could be very high, in a range of $2,000 to $5,000 for families) is likely to cause a large number of families with relatively modest income to fall into the category of being "underinsured": they are at increased risk (especially when including premiums and health care expenses not even covered by their policy) of having out-of-pocket costs exceeding 10 percent of their income. This concern is aggravated by the fact

that many costs (e.g., charges that exceed allowed rate levels, charges for non-covered services) will not count toward meeting the deductible or toward any stop-loss in the policy. In our view, shifting this kind of financial burden to families with moderate incomes is undesirable. This segment of the population is also at risk of facing loss of employer coverage (if employers drop out of the health care market) and higher premiums for low-deductible coverage (if high-deductible policies are available).

Focusing on transforming our health care marketplace into a high-deductible marketplace is a dangerous distraction from the urgent national goal of extending affordable, quality health coverage to all.

"To achieve the goal of reducing overall health care costs while improving quality ... Medicare Advantage is providing very important options to Medicare beneficiaries."

Medicare Private Insurance Improves Health Care Quality and Reduces Costs

Mark McClellan

In the following viewpoint, Mark McClellan explains the efficiency and value of Medicare Advantage (MA) health plans. These plans allow those who are eligible for Medicare (government health insurance) to opt instead to receive health care through private insurers that are paid by Medicare. The enrollees typically choose a doctor from a select network. The primary physician encourages preventative medicine and makes recommendations for specialized care. The physician's knowledge of his or her patients ideally will lead to lower medical costs by avoiding unnecessary treatments or care. Original Medicare patients are not restricted to specific physicians and can seek help from any doctor or hospital that accepts Medicare, but they may

Mark McClellan, Testimony on Medicare Advantage and the Federal Budget, House Budget Committee, U.S. Congress, June 28, 2007.

face higher fee-for-service costs. McClellan states that the lower costs of service are one of the benefits of MA plans. He also contends that the focus on preventative care improves the health of MA members and cuts down on costs. Mark McClellan is a senior fellow at the Brooking Institution, an independent public policy research organization, and the director of that institution's Engelberg Center for Health Care Reform.

As you read, consider the following questions:

1. What are some of the preventative services that MA members receive, as McClellan lists them?
2. According to McClellan, how does drug coverage in MA plans compare to that of Original Medicare?
3. As McClellan reports, how much can MA enrollees save in out-of-pocket costs each year as compared to Original Medicare recipients?

Before discussing the efficiency of Medicare Advantage [MA] plans, I would like to start with a comment on the importance of considering *value*—which is the way economists define efficiency—in the context of our health care system. Economic efficiency is not simply reducing costs to the government. For example, consider two kinds of health care coverage. One kind generally pays for complications of health problems after they happen, but limits coverage of preventive care, services to help people with chronic diseases stay well, and other benefits that improve health, resulting in higher costs to patients. The other kind of coverage is more in line with 21st-century health care: it provides more personalized medical services, such as helping people understand their risk factors, comply with drug therapies and other treatments to prevent complications, avoid duplicative services, and as a result it achieves better health outcomes. Even if these two kinds of coverage cost the same amount to the government, they are by no means equally efficient. Because the latter type of coverage achieves better quality for the same amount of government payment—because it delivers greater value—it is the more efficient approach. In fact, even if the more up-to-date coverage were somewhat more costly, because it delivers better health, it may still be the more efficient plan. Moreover, economic efficiency cannot be determined simply by looking at costs to the government. Efficiency depends on overall costs, including costs paid by beneficiaries as well as the government. Coverage that shifts costs to beneficiaries without lowering overall costs—or perhaps increasing them—does not increase efficiency.

If we want to achieve a high-value, efficient health care system, then Federal policies must encourage high-value health care. With this background in mind, I would like to describe how the Medicare Advantage program overall is performing.

Medicare Advantage Provides
High-Quality Care

Overall, compared to fee-for-service Medicare, beneficiaries in Medicare Advantage plans have much lower out-of-pocket costs; they receive significantly more preventive benefits, drug coverage, and services to help them better manage their chronic diseases; they have very high satisfaction rates; and in most cases, their overall care costs (Medicare plus beneficiary) are lower.

For example, Medicare Advantage beneficiaries receive preventive services like mammograms, colorectal cancer screening, prostate screening, and immunizations at significantly higher rates than beneficiaries in traditional fee-for-service (FFS) Medicare. In addition, compared to other Medicare beneficiaries without supplemental "Medigap" coverage, MA beneficiaries are only one-third as likely (6 percent versus 17 percent) to report delaying the use of needed care due to cost. . . .

Importantly, MA plans are also providing drug coverage that is more extensive and much less costly than in traditional

The Two Ways to Receive Medicare Coverage

Original Medicare Plan

> **Part A (Hospital)**

> **Part B (Medical)**

Medicare provides this coverage. Part B is optional. You have your choice of doctors. Your costs may be higher than in Medicare Advantage Plans.

> **Part D (Prescription Drug Coverage)**

You can choose this coverage. Private companies approved by Medicare run these plans. Plans cover different drugs. Medically necessary drugs must be covered.

> **Medigap (Medicare Supplement Insurance) Policy**

You can choose to buy this private coverage (or an employer/union may offer similar coverage) to fill in gaps in Part A and Part B coverage. Costs vary by policy and company.

> **OR**

> **Medicare Advantage Plans like HMOs and PPOs**

> **Called "Part C," this option combines your Part A (Hospital) and Part B (Medical)**

Private insurance companies approved by Medicare provide this coverage. Generally, you must see doctors in the plan. Your costs may be lower than in the Original Medicare Plan, and you may get extra benefits.

> **Part D (Prescription Drug Coverage)**

Most Part C plans cover prescription drugs. If they don't, you may be able to choose this coverage. Plans cover different drugs. Medically necessary drugs must be covered.

Centers for Medicare & Medicaid Services,
Medicare & You, 2007.

FFS Medicare. This difference in generosity and cost, which increased between 2006 and 2007 and may continue to increase in the future, is likely the result of several factors. First, most MA plans can manage the use of prescription drugs more effectively, as part of their efforts to support the overall coordination of care for a patient's health. Second, higher compliance with drugs has been shown to reduce other health care costs, and because MA plans have incentives to keep overall costs down that do not exist in traditional FFS, they can capture the savings in hospital, physician, and other costs from the greater compliance that comes with more comprehensive drug coverage. Again, this is a more efficient approach to health care coverage.

Finally, most MA plans provide much more support for patients with chronic diseases than is available in traditional FFS Medicare. This is critically important, since the vast majority of costs in Medicare—and most of the cost growth in Medicare—relates to treating the complications of a limited number of serious chronic diseases. Our health care system has huge and persisting quality gaps in the prevention and treatment of chronic diseases. There is no population in this country that needs such personalized services to improve coordination and prevent complications from chronic diseases more than Medicare beneficiaries.

All of these features—better preventive care, lower out-of-pocket costs, better drug coverage, better support for quality care for chronic diseases—are signs of more efficient health care. Not surprisingly, they add up to very large savings for beneficiaries—on average, out-of-pocket costs are $86 a month less in MA, compared to traditional FFS Medicare with Medigap (counting beneficiary premiums) or no supplemental coverage. That's more than $1000 a year in savings. This is why a recent analysis by Adam Atherly and Ken Thorpe of Emory University concluded that even though MA payments increase Medicare costs, "the size of the increase in costs will be less than the value of the supplemental benefits provided to beneficiaries"—that is, overall costs to beneficiaries and the Federal government are lower in the MA plans. . . .

Encouraging Coordination and Efficiency

To achieve the goal of reducing overall health care costs while improving quality—that is, to improve efficiency from the standpoint of our overall health care system, and to spend beneficiary as well as tax dollars more effectively—Medicare Advantage is providing very important options to Medicare beneficiaries.

If our nation is going to close the huge gap in prevention and in quality of care for chronic diseases, it is essential that we promote access to coverage like that available in most MA plans, which emphasizes preventing illness in the first place, avoiding preventable complications of chronic diseases, and using health services more efficiently. As Administrator of CMS [Centers for Medicare & Medicaid Services], I was a strong supporter of greater prevention and greater focus on prevention and improving care for chronic diseases within the traditional Medicare program as well. Over the past several years, CMS has implemented many steps in traditional FFS Medicare to improve quality and efficiency. These steps include a major "My Health, My Medicare" prevention initiative to encourage beneficiaries to take advantage of the expanded coverage of preventive services, the Medicare Health Support program to pilot the availability of disease and care management programs in traditional FFS Medicare, and initial steps toward providing better information on quality and efficiency and paying more for better care not just more care, to encourage better health and greater efficiency. But progress has been slow, because it is challenging to encourage the kinds of care coordination and integration that promote quality and efficiency, and that get the right care to the right patient at the right time, in an FFS payment system. In contrast, . . . most

MA plans have clearly demonstrated the capacity to achieve higher levels of quality without increasing overall health care costs, and in many cases reducing overall costs. . . .

The best solution to Medicare's financing problems isn't to take away innovative coverage options and shift costs to beneficiaries—particularly those with limited means who are struggling with out-of-pocket costs today. There are better ways to address the long-term sustainability of the Medicare program while promoting more efficient health care.

| "Private health plans often fail to deliver what they promise."

Medicare Private Insurance Does Not Improve Health Care Quality or Reduce Costs

Medicare Rights Center

Founded in 1989, the Medicare Rights Center (MRC) is the largest independent source of health care information and assistance in the United States for people with Medicare. The MRC argues in the following viewpoint that Medical Advantage (MA) private health insurance plans cost more than Original Medicare health plans and have problems concerning quality of care. As the MRC explains, out-of-pocket expenses may be higher for MA participants because private insurers have no incentive to keep costs down. Private plans also dictate what doctors a patient can see and have been known to deny coverage to patients who seek emergency care outside their provider network. The MRC maintains that MA plans are not delivering on their promise of better, more cost-effective care.

Medicare Rights Center, "Too Good to Be True: The Fine Print in Medicare Private Health Plan Benefits," *www.Medicarerights.org*, April, 2007. © 2007 by Medicare Rights Center. Reproduced by permission. www.medicarerights.org.

As you read, consider the following questions:

1. According to the MRC, about what percentage of Medicare recipients choose to remain with Original Medicare plans?

2. The MRC notes that some private insurers use excess subsidies to fund dental and vision plans for their MA recipients. Why does the MRC believe this may not be to the recipient's benefit?

3. If a person joins an MA program and is dissatisfied with service, how long does the MRC say he or she normally has to wait before switching back to another type of plan?

Nearly 8.3 million of the 43 million Americans with Medicare receive their medical care through private insurance companies, also called Medicare Advantage (MA) plans. The government pays the private insurance companies between 12 and 19 percent more than it would cost Medicare to serve the same people, according to the Medicare Payment Advisory Commission (MedPAC), a nonpartisan, independent federal body that advises the U.S. Congress on issues affecting the Medicare program. The non-partisan Congressional Budget Office estimates that the government's cost for these extra payments will amount to $65 billion over the next five years.

Are private plans worth it?

The [George W.] Bush administration and its supporters in Congress claim the extra money is a good investment because private insurers offer more generous benefits than Original Medicare. Their view closely echoes the insurance industry's assertion, in the words of its trade group President Karen Ignagni, that private plans "demonstrate their value to Medicare beneficiaries by providing better benefits at lower out-of-pocket costs."

Yet at a hearing held in March [2007] by the House Ways and Means health subcommittee, Acting Medicare Administrator Leslie Norwalk said that the agency has no data on what services people in private plans actually receive—only what the plans promise. Representative Pete Stark, the California Democrat who heads the subcommittee, reminded Ms. Norwalk that in order for private plan members to "enjoy" the benefits she praised, people have to be able to use them.

The experience of the Medicare Rights Center (MRC) helping people with Medicare get the health care they need shows that private health plans often fail to deliver what they promise. Plan members encounter an obstacle course when trying to get care and coverage, and they may pay more out-of-pocket costs than what they would have in Original Medicare. . . .

How Medicare Private Health Plans Work

People with Medicare can choose to get medical care directly from the government-administered Original Medicare program or from private insurance companies under contract with Medicare. More than 80 percent choose the Original Medicare program. Nineteen percent have enrolled in a Medicare private health plan.

Original Medicare has a standard benefit package that covers medically necessary care members can receive from nearly any hospital or doctor in the country. Medicare Part A is hospital insurance that covers inpatient services, including skilled nursing facilities and hospice care. Medicare Part B is medical insurance that covers outpatient services, including doctor visits, lab tests, durable medical equipment and home health services. Most people get Part A for free, but pay a monthly Part B premium ($93.50 in 2007). Both Parts A and B have a deductible. Generally, people have to pay 20 percent of Medicare's approved amount for doctor services.

For people who choose to enroll in a Medicare private health plan, Medicare pays the private health plan a set amount every month for each member. Members may have to pay a monthly premium in addition to the Medicare Part B premium and generally pay a fixed amount (a copayment of $20, for example) every time they see a doctor. The copayment can be higher to see a specialist.

The private plans are required to offer a benefit "package" that is at least as good as Medicare's and cover everything Medicare covers, but they do not have to cover every benefit in the same way. Plans that pay less than Medicare for some benefits, like skilled nursing facility care, can balance their benefits package by offering lower copayments for doctor visits. Private plans use some of the excess payments they receive from the government for each enrollee to offer supplemental benefits. Some plans put a limit on their members' annual out-of-pocket spending on medical care, providing some insurance against catastrophic costs over $5,000, for example. But many plans use the excess subsidies to offer dental coverage and other services not covered by Medicare and leave members exposed to high medical bills if they fall seriously ill. No one can foresee what type of care they may need in six months. Private plan members can end up with unexpectedly high out-of-pocket costs. And plans that do have a limit on out-of-pocket costs generally are not advertising that benefit, probably because it would attract sicker (and less profitable) members who need more costly care.

Costs to Consumers

In Original Medicare, people can buy supplemental insurance to cover Medicare deductibles and coinsurance, which makes their out-of-pocket costs fairly predictable regardless of what medical care they may need. People with low incomes may be eligible for assistance programs, like the Qualified Medicare Beneficiary (QMB) or Medicaid, to cover those costs. People in private health plans, on the other hand, cannot get supplemental coverage for the unexpected out-of-pocket costs they may have to face if they become seriously ill with the "wrong" disease for their plan. . . .

In addition, out-of-pocket costs in private plans can rise substantially from year to year. For example, a study released by AARP [American Association of Retired Persons] in November 2006 found that the average unweighted facility cost for a three-day hospitalization in Medicare private health plans increased 37 percent between 2002 and 2006; for a private health plan enrollee hospitalized for two six-day stays and one three-day stay, the cost increased 59 percent over the same period. In both scenarios, the private health plan rate of increase was substantially higher than the 17 percent increase in the Original Medicare hospital deductible over the same four-year period.

Some Medicare private health plans also offer case and disease management, nurse advice lines and utilization management. The Center for Studying Health System Change has been monitoring these services since 1996 as offered by commercial health plans in 12 cities. The group's experts found no "credible evidence on what impact they have on costs, quality and outcomes."

In Congressional testimony [in April 2007], Peter Orszag, the director of the Congressional Budget Office, noted that private insurers have higher administrative costs than the government Medicare program "because of their smaller scale of operations and their costs associated with network development and retention, care management, marketing, and reinsurance."

The burden of high administrative costs (generally 10 to 15 percent for private health plans compared to 3 percent for Original Medicare) adds to the strong incentive private insurers have to limit access to benefits: members who do not use services cost companies less and increase profits. Orszag put it this way: "As a result, private plans can provide Medicare services at a lower cost than the FFS [fee for service] [Medicare] program only if they can achieve savings through lower utili-

---

True Story of Limited Benefits

Mr. R., who lives in a New York City suburb, was injured after he was hit by a car. His injuries included broken teeth and a broken jaw. Mr. R. could not eat solid food for seven years after the accident. He was unable to work and could not afford to pay his medical bills because his only income was his monthly Social Security Disability Insurance check. When Mr. R. became eligible for Medicare, he learned that Medicare does not cover dental care. Last year, he attended a meeting sponsored by Oxford and met with a sales representative who assured him that Oxford's SecureHorizons plan would cover the dental treatment he desperately needed. After he joined, he was denied dental care and was told that Oxford only pays for accident-related dental care within a year of the accident.

Medicare Rights Center, April 2007.

---

zation or reductions in payment rates for providers that more than offset their higher administrative costs."...

Medicare Private Health Care Problems

The problems people have in Medicare private health plans (also known as Medicare Advantage plans) are numerous. Many people discover these flaws only after they have joined the plan—and most cannot switch until the following year.

Most of the cases MRC handles fall into the following categories:

1. Care can cost more than it would under Original Medicare. Medicare private health plans are required to offer a benefit "package" that is at least as good as Medicare's, but they do not have to cover every benefit in the same way. For example, while Medicare covers 100 percent of the cost of care for the first 20 days a person requires skilled nursing facility care, a private plan can require members pay a copayment each day they are in a nursing home. Because of this, some people can pay more in a private plan than they would have under Original Medicare. . . .

2. Private plans are not stable. Unlike Medicare, which has offered guaranteed health care coverage since 1966, private health insurance companies come and go. Companies merge or go out of business. They change the benefits package from one year to the next, including what benefits they cover and what the benefits cost. All of these changes are outside the control of plan members, but they can affect their access to the care they need. . . .

3. Difficulty getting emergency or urgent care. No one knows when or where an accident or other medical emergency will strike. That is why Medicare law mandates that private plans cover emergency and urgent care regardless of whether the provider is in the plan's network or within the plan's service area. (Urgent care is a sudden illness or injury that needs immediate medical attention but is not life threatening.) However, MRC gets many calls from private health plan members who are being denied payment for out-of-network and even in-network emergency care or are being denied authorization to get urgent care while away from home. . . .

4. Continuity of care is broken. Health experts have long extolled the importance of continuity of care. This generally means the availability or constancy of the health care provider as the source of care, keeping follow-up appointments with the provider and planning seamlessness transitions when care changes from one setting to another. Knowledge of a patient's medical and family history and personal preferences are among the important information lost when people have to change their health care provider. Changing in the midst of a treatment can be traumatic and detrimental to the patient's health. . . .

5. Members have to follow plan rules to get covered care. Private health plans generally require that a member's doctor get permission from the plan (prior authorization) before a member get certain procedures, tests or care from a hospital or skilled nursing facility. If a member gets the care without the plan's permission, the plan can refuse to pay for it. If the plan denies prior authorization, the member needs to enlist the doctor's help in appealing the plan's decision in order to get the care. . . .

6. Choice of doctor, hospital, and other providers is restricted. . . . Unlike Original Medicare, most private health plans have a network of health care providers—doctors, hospitals, skilled nursing facilities and others—that members must use in order to receive full coverage (except in an emergency). Health Maintenance Organization (HMOs) generally will not pay for care members get from providers who are not part of the plan's network. Preferred Provider Organizations (PPOs) usually allow members to see providers outside the network, but they have to pay more out of their own pocket for the privilege. Private Fee-for-Service (PFFS) plans allow members to go to any provider that will accept the plan's terms and fees, but many providers will not.

Plan members may find they cannot go to the specialist or hospital recommended by their doctor, the nursing home they stayed at last time they needed skilled nursing facility care, or other providers of their choice. Problems arise when the provider is not in the plan's network, has dropped out of the network or is dropped from the network by the plan. To add to the problem, while health care providers can drop out of a plan's network at any time, members are usually locked in to the plan for a year. . . .

7. Difficulty getting care away from home. Many people with Medicare enjoy their retirement by spending time with family in other parts of the country or live part of the year in warmer/cooler climates. Original Medicare allows them to get covered health care anywhere in the country. Private health plans generally only allow members to get care within their service area (except in an emergency)....

8. Promised extra benefits can be very limited. People with Medicare who choose to enroll in a private plan often do so to get coverage of some benefits Medicare does not cover, like dental and vision care. These benefits vary widely from plan to plan. People sometimes find that the benefit they joined the plan to get will not cover as much as they thought it would.

9. People with both Medicare and Medicaid encounter higher costs. People with Medicare and Medicaid have virtually no out-of-pocket costs. Medicaid helps pay Medicare deductibles and coinsurance. However, if they join a Medicare private health plan, Medicaid may not help pay any of their out-of-pocket costs.

Failing to Deliver What Is Promised

Medicare private health plans were brought into the Medicare program with the promise that competition and entrepreneurship would lead to better, more cost-effective care. In helping people with Medicare get the health care they need, the Medicare Rights Center has found that all too often private health plans do not deliver what they promise. Even with enhanced payments, private health plans often fail to deliver coverage that a patient could obtain from Original Medicare. Medicare private health plans should not cost taxpayers more than Original Medicare. Congress should level the playing field by making private health plan payments equal 100 percent of what it costs to insure people in the Original Medicare program.

Periodical Bibliography

The following articles have been selected to supplement the diverse views presented in this chapter.

Laura Brasseur	"Medicare Physician Pay: A Fatally Flawed Formula," *Internal Medicine World Report*, April 2007.
Jonathan Cohn	"What's the One Thing Big Business and the Left Have in Common?" *New York Times Magazine*, April 1, 2007.
Avery Comarow	"What It Takes to Be the Best," *U.S. News & World Report*, July 23, 2007.
Consumer Reports	"False Promises: 'Consumer Driven' Health Plans," May 2006.
Matthew DoBias	"Docs vs. Insurers," *Modern Healthcare*, May 28, 2007.
Mike Huckabee	"Prevention in a Free Market," *Modern Healthcare*, July 16, 2007.
Maclean's	"Private Medical Care Is Here to Stay," May 1, 2006.
Daniel McGinn and Karen Springen	"Express-Lane Medicine," *Newsweek*, July 30, 2007.
National Right to Life News	"Tell Congress to Say NO to Health Care Rationing by Preserving the Private-Fee-For-Service Alternative to Medicare!" July 2007.
Kimberly J. Retzlaff	"Taking Control," *American Fitness*, January/ February 2007.
Thommy Thompson	"Quality Is In Our Hands," *Modern Healthcare*, July 30, 2007.
David Whelan	"Is There Another Doctor in the House?" *Forbes*, March 26, 2007.

How Should the Health Care System Be Altered to Help the Uninsured?

Chapter Preface

In the first week of January 2007, Senator Susan Collins of Maine and Senator Mary Landrieu of Louisiana put before Congress the Access to Affordable Health Care Act (S. 158). This act is aimed at expanding health care coverage to the 47 million Americans who lack insurance and the uncounted number of Americans who are underinsured. Collins notes that it is a poor assumption that most people who lack insurance are unemployed; she states in a 2006 editorial to a Maine newspaper that "as many as 83 percent of Americans who do not have health insurance are in a family with a worker."

Most of these uninsured workers are employed at small businesses that cannot afford the increases in health care costs and thus are liable to drop employee benefits. Through the Affordable Health Care Act, Collins and Landrieu propose to offer small businesses tax breaks that would allow them to provide coverage to their employees. The act also supplies grant money to start up small business co-ops with the express purpose of purchasing health insurance as a better-funded collective. Furthermore, the proposal gives individuals and families a tax break for putting money aside for long-term care of family members who might develop chronic illnesses or cognitive impairments.

Collins and Landrieu also wish to expand the State Child Health Insurance Program (SCHIP) which, according to them, has successfully insured millions of children in low-income families. Under the Affordable Health Care Act, states would be given the opportunity to use SCHIP funds to pay for health coverage for the parents as well as the children of eligible families. In addition, the act puts more money into community health centers and programs that stress preventative care.

Although this ambitious piece of legislation seems that it could have been born out of the rhetoric of tax incentives, preventative care, and expanding state programs that pervade the 2008 presidential race, Collins and Landrieu have in fact introduced a version of this bill into every session of Congress since 2000. Every year, the bill has been read and passed to committee where it languished until the session ended with no further action taken. Collins has asserted that because of the climate surrounding the presidential race, she expects that the Affordable Health Care Act will have a better chance of passing into law in 2007–2008. In the following chapter, other politicians and health care experts offer their views on the various plans put forth to address the swelling ranks of the uninsured in the United States.

> *"HSAs make a difference—are making health care more accessible to those without insurance."*

Health Savings Accounts Will Make Health Care More Affordable

George W. Bush

George W. Bush is the forty-third President of the United States. In 2003 the Bush administration implemented health savings accounts (HSAs) as part of the Medicare Prescription Drug, Improvement, and Modernization Act; the president has since succeeded in convincing Congress to expand these accounts to make them a viable alternative to traditional high-cost insurance coverage. In the following viewpoint, President Bush explains how HSAs give consumers control over how their health care dollars are spent so that they can become more discriminating users of health services and help bring down the cost of health care. Bush views HSAs as an essential part of making health care into a consumer-driven market in which services will compete for patients' dollars. This competition, he believes, will lower prices even further and make health care more affordable to all.

George W. Bush, President Discusses Health Care, Wendy's International, Inc., Dublin, Ohio, February 15, 2006. www.whitehouse.gov.

As you read, consider the following questions:

1. According to President Bush, why is there no incentive under traditional health insurance programs to lower costs?

2. What entities contribute to health savings accounts, according to the President?

3. In Bush's view, why are HSAs a good alternative for young people who lack insurance?

[In facing the nation's health care needs] the federal government obviously has a role, to make sure the Medicare system is cost-effective and works well, make sure Medicaid works well and gives flexibility to states, and to expand community health centers.

I now want to talk to you about how the rest of us need to have a health care system if you don't fall into those categories. What should the role of the government be? And I believe the role of the government ought to be to empower consumers to make choices. And so let me talk to you about five ideas I have to make sure that health care is more available and more affordable.

And the first one is to expand health savings accounts. I call them HSAs. When you hear me say HSA, that's kind of government-speak for health savings account. They—HSAs are helping to begin a movement away from what's called a third-party payer system to one where the consumer is very much involved in making wise purchases of health care. That's a very important philosophical point.

Unseen Costs

The traditional insurance today will cover your health care costs—most of your health care costs—in exchange for a high premium payment up front. The costs are generally shared by you and your employer. You may also pay a small deductible and co-payment at the time of treatment. What's interesting about this system is that those payments cover only a fraction of the actual costs of health care, the rest of which are picked up by a third party, basically your insurance company.

It means most Americans have no idea what their actual cost of treatment is. You show up, you got a traditional plan, you got your down payment, you pay a little co-pay, but you have no idea what the cost is. Somebody else pays it for you. And so there's no reason at all to kind of worry about price. If somebody else is paying the bill, you just kind of—hey, it seems like a pretty good deal. There's no pressure for an industry to lower price. And so what you're seeing is price going up. If you don't care what you're paying, and the provider doesn't have any incentive to lower, the natural inclination is for the cost to go up and the insurance companies, sure enough, pass on the costs—the increase in cost to you and your employer. That's what's happening.

The fundamental problem with traditional coverage is that there's no incentive to control how their health care dollars are spent. You don't have any incentive, whatsoever. And that's one of the cost drivers in our system. If we want to solve health care problems, if we want to make health care affordable and available, we've got to analyze and address the cost drivers of health care. And there's one right there. If patients controlled how their health care dollars are spent, the result is better treatment at lower cost.

An Example of Market-Driven Treatment

I'll give you an interesting example of a procedure called LASIK—laser eye surgeries. It's a good example of how the market can work when there's not a third-party payer involved. You might remember when LASIK first appeared, was approved about a decade ago for its use. It went through the process of getting government approval, and when approved it was an opportunity for people to have their eyesight—feeling a little nervous about LASIK surgery when it first came out, and it was awfully expensive. Consumers began to, however, inquire as to why something costs the way it costs, how safe it was; doctors felt more comfortable starting to offer more and more of the surgery; more providers came in the market, there was transparency of pricing. You might—I can remember billboards springing up with people advertising LASIK surgery. Today the price of LASIK surgery has dropped dramatically. More people are getting the surgery—they're giving up their glasses and contact lenses.

The market is working. I think if you go back and look at the history of the pricing of LASIK surgery, the availability of LASIK surgery, you'll find that when consumers start showing up saying, I want to know information, I'm interested in this idea, how about—how does your cost compare to old Joe's over here—the market began to adjust. LASIK surgery is now more widespread, at much more reasonable cost for consumers.

And so, how to affect those kinds of cost changes in the health care industry—that's what we're really here to discuss. And one way to do so is to—to make health care more responsive is through health savings accounts. Many people in our country don't know what a health savings account is. I will start to try to explain it here.

The Elements of an HSA

First, it is a part of our drive to make health care more consumer-driven. There's two components to a health savings account; one is low-cost catastrophic insurance coverage, and a tax-free health savings account. Those are the two components of what I'm talking about. Catastrophic coverage protects you and the family in the event of devastating medical illness—if you're really sick, a catastrophic plan kicks in.

The health savings account portion of this product allows you and your employer to contribute tax-free to pay for routine medical costs. In other words, your company, or yourself, or a combination of the two makes a tax-free contribution into a health savings plan, a savings plan that you own. It's yours to call your own. And the savings within that plan are tax-free. In other words, you're not just going to put it under your pillow, you put it into a bank until you use it. The interest will be tax-free. Your money is growing.

It means that if you don't spend money in your savings account on health care, you can roll it over to the next year, tax-free. You have money growing for health care to pay incidental expenses; it's growing at a reasonable interest rate; it's yours you call your own, and if you don't spend it in a year you can put it into the next year, and the next year, and the next year.

For many routine medical needs, HSAs mean you can shop around until you get the best treatment for the best price. In other words, it's your money; you're responsible for routine medical expenses; the insurance pays for the catastrophic care. You're responsible for paying for the portion of your health care costs up to your deductible. And so you— you talk to your doctor, you say, can't we find this drug at a little cheaper cost? Or you go to a specialist, maybe we can do this a little better—old Joe does it for X, I'm going—why don't you try it for Y? It allows you to choose treatment or tests that meet your needs in a way that you're comfortable with when it comes to paying the bills. In other words, decisions about routine medical treatments are made by you and the doc, not by third-party people that you never know. And all of a sudden, when you inject this type of thinking in the system, price starts to matter. You're aware of price. You begin to say, well, maybe there's a better way to do this, and more cost-effective way.

The combined cost of catastrophic insurance coverage and HSA contributions are usually less expensive than traditional coverage. That's important to know. In other words, HSAs are making health care more affordable. . . .

A Good Alternative for the Uninsured

Forty percent of those who own HSAs have family incomes below $50,000 a year. In other words, if people are having trouble affording traditional insurance, all of a sudden the HSA becomes a more affordable product. HSAs make a difference—are making health care more accessible to those without insurance. In the first year HSAs were available, more than a third of those who bought HSAs had been uninsured. In other words, as health care becomes more affordable, it makes it easier, obviously, for somebody who is uninsured to be able to pick up health insurance.

You know, a lot of young folks are uninsured. You might remember the days when you kind of felt like you were never going to get sick. So why should you buy insurance? Why do you need coverage? A lot of young folks are saying, wait a minute, this is a pretty good deal. If I'm going to stay healthy and can save a portion of that money, tax-free, and I'm not going to spend money on health care for a while, all of a sudden a nest egg really begins to build. By the way, it's a nest egg they call their own, not something the government—if there's excess money in your account, the government can't take it away, or insurance can't take it away, it's yours. You own the thing. It's—a vital part of kind of a responsible society is when there's a sense of ownership in important parts of our economy.

[Since early 2005], the number of HSAs has tripled. In other words, people are becoming aware. . . . I want people to be aware of it. The number of people who bought HSAs has gone from a million to 3 million. I'm going to talk today about ways to make sure that HSAs are—even expand even further.

You know, I can remember the debate in Washington—I'm sure you can, as well—I remember one person who said, health savings accounts are not a solution for the uninsured, they're regressive, they favor the wealthy. It's just not the facts.

HSAs Provide Choice

Health Savings Accounts are a good thing for our citizens, and they are a good thing for the economy. HSAs will make health insurance less expensive in the long run, which is the best thing we can do to tackle the problem of the uninsured in this country. They will make the health care sector of our economy more user-friendly and more efficient. They will give workers more choice and more flexibility in their choice of plans, and in deciding where they want to work. In short, they would help to bring our health care system into the new economy.

Orrin Hatch, Statement before U.S. Senate, February 6, 2006.

They've helped the uninsured, and a lot of folks with incomes under $50,000 are buying these plans. It's kind of basically saying, if you're not making a lot of money you can't make decisions for yourself. That's kind of a Washington attitude, isn't it—we'll decide for you, you can't figure it out yourself. I think a lot of folks ... would argue that point of view is just simply backwards and not true. ...

Making HSAs More Attractive

I'm going to talk about three ways to make them more attractive, so more people can have the benefits of an HSA, like ... the small business owners we've had. The greatest obstacle— one of the greatest obstacles to expansion of HSAs is the tax code. One problem is that under current law, employers and employees pay no income or payroll tax on any health insurance provided through the workplace. ... It's a benefit that's not taxable. Those who buy their insurance on their own don't get the same tax break. That means that the self-employed, the unemployed, and workers at companies that do not provide insurance are at a disadvantage. The playing field isn't level. And so I believe that one thing Congress needs to do is to give Americans who purchase their own HSA policies the same tax breaks as those who get their health insurance from their employers.

Another problem is that under current law, the amount you can put into your HSA tax-free is limited to the amount of your deductible. But sometimes your out-of-pocket expenses are greater than your deductible. That's because on some catastrophic plans, there is an additional co-pay and, therefore, when you—you're paying after-tax dollars under the current law if you exceed the amount of money you spend beyond your deductible. We can change that. We can raise the cap on the amount of money you put into your HSA so it remains tax-free, so that all out-of-pocket expenses can be covered. [The cap was raised in 2007 to $2,850 for individuals, $5,650 for families.]

And finally, HSAs—we want to make sure they meet the practical needs of today's workers. I told you people are changing jobs. And one of the problems is, a lot of folks fear that when they choose jobs, they're going to lose their health care. And that means—people feel like they've got to get locked into a job because of health care. And that's not right. They need to be more thoughtful to our workers, and recognize that this is a changing world in which we live. And so we ought to make sure people can take their own health savings account with them job to job.

Today the savings in your health account—health savings account are portable—portable means you can take it job to job. So you've got savings in your own account, you can take it with you. But the health insurance that comes with the account you can't take with you, because of outdated laws and practices that prevent insurers from offering portable policies. So I believe that health insurers should be allowed to sell portable HSA policies nationwide.

You see, it's like car insurance. If you change jobs, you can take your car insurance with you. You can't take your insurance in your HSA with you. In order to make sure this economy works better, in order to make sure the health care system functions better for our workers, we've got to make sure portability in HSAs is consistent and real. It's going to make a difference in people's lives when Congress gets that done.

| "[Health savings accounts] place a strain on the consumers who can least afford, and most need, health insurance, while the rich and healthy benefit."

Health Savings Accounts Will Not Make Health Care More Affordable

Families USA

Families USA is a national nonprofit, nonpartisan organization dedicated to the achievement of high-quality, affordable health care for all Americans. In the following viewpoint, the organization asserts that health savings accounts (HSAs) are an inappropriate response to the health care crisis in America. Families USA argues that the low up-front costs of HSAs makes them attractive, but the poor would not likely be able to meet the monthly contributions without straining household finances, and they would never be able to afford the high deductibles if a health emergency occurred. Because of the need to build up a good amount of savings in these accounts, lower-income participants would also be less inclined to seek routine medical treatment for fear of draining what money had accrued, Families

Families USA, "HSAs: Missing the Target," Washington, DC: 2006. © 2006 Families USA. Reproduced by permission. November 2006. www.familiesusa.org.

USA contends. Furthermore, the organization notes that the wise use of HSAs depends on the concept of shopping around for cheaper medical care, but few Americans have the knowledge or time to do this effectively, especially if a medical emergency is taking place.

As you read, consider the following questions:

1. Why do most Americans lack the essential information to make decisions about health care quality and cost, according to Families USA?
2. Why does the organization argue that lowering consumer spending (through the adoption of HSAs) would not make a significant dent in health care costs?
3. If HSAs become popular enough, what does Families USA say will happen to the older and less-healthy people who stick with traditional insurance plans?

HSAs and their companion high-deductible health plans are often touted as affordable health insurance alternatives for the uninsured. As President [George W.] Bush said in a 2004 speech, "HSAs will make it easier for some people who are now uninsured to purchase health insurance." The facts show, however, that HSAs are not affordable options for the uninsured and are thus unlikely to significantly reduce the overall number of uninsured Americans.

- The vast majority of uninsured Americans have low incomes: One-third of the uninsured earn less than $25,000 a year, and another one-third earn between $25,000 and $50,000 a year.

- Most uninsured Americans would be unable to save large amounts of money to put into HSAs: Because most low-income people have little disposable income left after paying for housing, food, and other necessities, it is unlikely that they could manage to save enough money in their HSA to even cover the deductible—a minimum of $1,050 for an individual or $2,100 for a family. Some families would need to save as much as $10,500 to pay their deductibles and cost-sharing, or even more if they required services that were not covered by their plans.

• The tax subsidy that supports HSAs is too small to reach people with low incomes: Those at the bottom of the income scale who are too poor to pay federal income taxes would receive *no* subsidy. And those with slightly higher incomes who fall in the lowest tax bracket would receive a mere 10 cents for every dollar they put into an HSA. Thus, the HSA tax break offers low-income people too small a subsidy to enable them to sign up for an HSA.

HSAs Are Not an Effective Way to Control Costs

The Administration has praised HSAs for many reasons, but primarily as a way to contain health care costs. In *The Economic Report of the President*, HSAs coupled with high-deductible health plans are touted as an alternative to comprehensive coverage that "dull[s] the incentives for consumers to shop carefully for cost-effective health care." The report continues, "By giving consumers both the incentives and the information needed to become better shoppers for health care, public policy can help control the growth in health care costs and improve the efficiency of the use of health care resources." However, there are several flies in this ointment.

• HSAs may induce consumers to skip necessary services, leading to higher costs in the long run: HSAs put consumers in the position of choosing between keeping money in their pockets and paying to see the doctor. Research has repeatedly shown that even modest increases in cost-sharing lead to consumers using fewer preventive and necessary services. Low-income people are even less likely to seek care if they must pay the full bill. They reduce their use of essential drugs, for example, and this leads to serious health problems and to increased use of emergency rooms. When consumers wait until they are very sick to seek treatment, health care costs rise significantly. In fact, a 2005 survey found that, due to the cost, enrollees in high-deductible health plans were significantly more likely to delay or go without health care when they were sick than were enrollees in comprehensive plans.

- Individual consumers have little ability to reduce provider costs: HSA proponents further argue that making consumers shop for less expensive care will create competition among health care providers, forcing them to reduce their charges. This theory, however, is flawed. Individual consumers do not have the market clout needed to obtain the lowest prices. It is doubtful that doctors and hospitals will reduce charges beyond the discounted rates insurance companies have already negotiated with them.

- Individual consumers cannot "comparison shop" for health care: Shopping for quality, affordable health care is simply not a reasonable option for the vast majority of Americans for a variety of reasons, including lack of knowledge, time, and available information:

- Shopping for health care is not like shopping for a cheap television. Consumers shopping for electronics may be willing to accept some sacrifice in quality for a cheaper price, but no health care consumer wants to accept low-quality care.

While consumers will check prices at a number of retailers to find the best price before buying, someone having a possible heart attack should not be expected to call around to hospitals looking for the lowest price tag for treatment. Consumers lack the specialized knowledge required to choose among health care options. Essential information about health care quality and cost is unavailable to most consumers, so they will not have the information needed to make informed choices. A 2005 survey showed that very few high-deductible plans (including those that can be used with an HSA) provided any information about the cost or quality of doctor or hospital services. Furthermore, making cost information more widely available may not solve the problem: Some economists hold that publicizing the prices that hospitals offer insurers (including those charged under high-deductible plans) may actually cause hospital prices to increase.

For many consumers, language barriers make shopping for care extremely difficult: About 45 million Americans have limited English proficiency. Most of those with limited English proficiency are Latino and Asian, and these numbers are increasing.

- Without the necessary information, consumers will not be able to protect their health while reducing the cost of their health care through "smart shopping."

- Increasing consumer exposure to health care costs will net little in cost savings: Even if HSAs succeed in curbing consumer spending on health care, the savings would be trivial compared to total health care spending. Many analysts, including the Congressional Research Service and the Administration itself, have reached this conclusion. People with chronic conditions account for the vast majority of total health care spending, but they have little in the way of flexibility to shop for cheaper care. According to the Tax Policy Center, 95 percent of all medical expenditures from insured households would exceed HSA deductibles. Since there's no incentive for consumers to bargain hunt after they've reached their deductible, there's no reason to think HSAs will have a cost-cutting effect on 95 percent of medical spending. Ironically, the only way for HSAs to have a real effect on cost containment would be to drastically increase the minimum deductible so more households would face the pressure to save money.

HSAs Are Inequitable and Will Harm Many Consumers

While it is doubtful that HSAs can achieve the positive goals of curbing health care costs and reducing the number of uninsured Americans, there are additional "unintended consequences" of HSAs that are cause for concern.

- Racial and ethnic minorities suffer disproportionately from chronic conditions and are thus less likely to benefit from HSAs: For example, African Americans and Latinos are twice as likely to suffer from diabetes as whites. Since racial and ethnic minorities are more likely to have acute or chronic conditions and are more likely to have low incomes, they are far less likely to benefit from HSAs and far more likely to be harmed by the high deductibles in the associated health plans.

- The HSA tax subsidy disproportionately rewards those who least need help: The tax deduction for contributions to an HSA account amounts to an indirect subsidy from the federal government. This subsidy gives the most to those who need it the least—those with higher incomes—and offers the least to the majority of uninsured people who have lower incomes. A dollar placed in a health savings account saves 35 cents for a person in the 35 percent tax bracket, while it saves just 10 cents for a person in the 10 percent tax bracket.

- HSAs may induce consumers to skip *necessary* health care services: As noted previously, HSAs encourage many consumers to delay or forgo treatment, which can be harmful to their health. This is particularly true for people with low incomes, who have less ability to absorb higher up-front costs.

- Rather than reducing overall costs, HSAs provide employers with a new way to pass cost increases on to workers: For families, deductibles for plans that can be used with HSAs range from $2,100 to $10,500 in 2006, and there is no guarantee that employers will help fill this hole. In 2006, 37 percent of employers who offered high-deductible plans contributed nothing to their employees' HSAs, leaving workers to meet the high deductibles on their own. And when employers did contribute, their contribution generally fell far short of the plan's deductible. One survey found that, among employers who did contribute, the average contribution was $988 for single coverage and $1,632 for family coverage. The average deductible in an employer-sponsored plan that can be used with an HSA was $2,011 for single coverage and $4,008 for family coverage in 2006. And even after they have met their deductibles, people in high-deductible health plans face other out-of-pocket costs: They may be charged copayments, and they must pay the full cost of any care that is not covered by their health plans. Rather than reducing costs, HSAs and high-deductible health plans simply shift the burden of health care costs from employers to workers.

- As young and healthy employees switch to HSAs, health insurance will become too costly for older and less healthy employees: Employees who are not in perfect health cannot afford the high out-of-pocket costs of the high-deductible plans that must be used with HSAs. Given a choice, they would likely remain in traditional

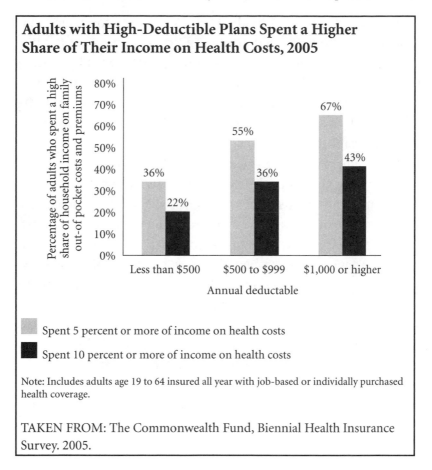

Adults with High-Deductible Plans Spent a Higher Share of Their Income on Health Costs, 2005

Percentage of adults who spent a high share of household income on family out-of pocket costs and premiums

Annual deductable

Spent 5 percent or more of income on health costs

Spent 10 percent or more of income on health costs

Note: Includes adults age 19 to 64 insured all year with job-based or individually purchased health coverage.

TAKEN FROM: The Commonwealth Fund, Biennial Health Insurance Survey. 2005.

plans, while many of their healthier coworkers would switch to HSAs. Thus, less-healthy employees will be grouped together in traditional plans, which will result in increased premiums for those plans. Many employers would then choose to drop traditional plans rather than pay these higher premiums. HSAs, therefore, may actually *increase* the number of Americans without health insurance.

HSAs Are a Radical Threat to Our Current Health Insurance System

HSAs threaten our nation's existing health insurance system. The basic concept that underlies health insurance is the pooling together of many individuals' risks in order to ensure that none are left unprotected from the costs of treating a catastrophic illness. Our current system pools people through their workplace. While not a perfect pooling mechanism, our employer-based system helps protect older and sicker individuals from higher health care costs by pooling them with younger, healthier coworkers.

By design, HSAs are attractive to the young, the healthy, and the wealthy. HSAs therefore increase the likelihood that these same individuals, whose lower health care costs balance out overall health care costs in traditional insurance plans, will enroll in high-deductible plans with HSAs so they can take advantage of the tax benefits. Consequently, older, poorer, and sicker individuals—who either do not make enough to benefit from the tax incentives of HSAs, cannot afford the high out-of-pocket costs necessary to enroll in high-deductible plans, or both—will remain in traditional, low-deductible insurance plans. Therefore, isolating the sickest and poorest in one pool—without the youngest and healthiest to help balance costs—will result in substantial increases in premiums for the population most at risk and least able to pay.

- Wealthier individuals are more likely than others to enroll in HSAs: When given a choice between an HSA with a high-deductible health plan and a comprehensive plan, wealthier people are the ones that choose high-deductible plans. For example, Federal Employees Health Benefits Program (FEHBP) enrollees who chose high-deductible health plans in 2005 were about twice as likely to have incomes of $75,000 or more as were those who enrolled in more traditional, comprehensive health plans. As mentioned earlier, wealthier individuals stand to earn at least twice as much in tax breaks from HSAs as people with modest incomes—a family of four with $40,000 in income would get a $470 tax break for depositing $4,000 in an HSA, but a similar family with

$120,000 in income would enjoy a $1,240 tax break for putting the same $4,000 into an HSA. And of course, the higher-income family will have a much easier time setting aside this amount. In fact, HSA marketing materials often stress HSAs' value as a tax shelter (rather than as a vehicle to pay for health care) and show how much people will gain over time through both tax breaks and interest.

- Healthier individuals are more likely to enroll in the high-deductible plans that can be used with HSAs: High-deductible plans only pay off if the consumer does not expect to have many medical expenses. Only healthy people are likely to take that risk.

- As wealthier and healthier individuals move into HSAs, traditional coverage will become more expensive: As younger and healthier consumers move into high-deductible plans, older and less healthy consumers will be left in traditional plans, driving up the costs of these plans. Research indicates that this rise in costs could be immediate and significant. Either the older and less healthy workers will be stuck with higher costs, or employers will drop their traditional plans—forcing older and sicker workers into less favorable HSA plans, into the individual market, or into the growing ranks of the uninsured.

- HSAs drain valuable dollars from the health care system: As wealthier and healthier Americans save money by switching to HSAs, less money will flow into the nation's health care system. HSAs allow healthy people to move their health care dollars into their non-health care budgets. Yet the overall amount of health care services Americans need will not be reduced. Unfortunately, that gaping hole in available dollars needed to support our health care system will have to be filled, and the burden may fall on those who do need, and must pay for, health care (either through their insurance premiums or directly). The bottom line is that there will be less money in the health care system, and that money will have to be recouped through higher overall prices for health care for everyone.

HSAs Create More Problems Than They Solve

HSAs do not solve the problems they were supposedly created to solve—the rising cost of health insurance and the growing number of uninsured. Instead, they place a strain on the consumers who can least afford, and most need, health insurance, while the rich and healthy benefit. Under current law (without considering the impact of additional changes now being considered that would make premiums for high-deductible plans tax-deductible). HSAs will cost our nation $17.1 billion in lost income taxes from the five-year period from 2007–2011. HSAs represent a radical change in our health care system that will drain money from our nation's budget without solving any of the very serious problems facing our current system.

> *"The president's plan would extend the tax exemption for health insurance to 18 million Americans who now buy coverage on their own, and to as many as 46 million more who have no insurance at all."*

Tax Deductions on Health Benefits Will Help the Uninsured

Michael F. Cannon

In the following viewpoint, Michael F. Cannon supports President George W. Bush's call to reduce taxes on health benefits so that more people would be inclined to purchase affordable private coverage. Cannon argues that people who buy consumer-based coverage are not receiving the tax break afforded those who receive coverage through employers. The latter group—that has most of its health care paid for by insurance—has no incentive to consume less insurance and keep costs down. These people should be limited on the amount of insurance premiums they can deduct from their taxes each year, Cannon claims. If this tax benefit was limited, more people might take advantage of cheaper health savings accounts or other private insurance, Cannon states, thus making insurance more affordable to all. Michael F. Cannon is director of health policy studies at the Cato Institute, a libertarian public policy research organization.

As you read, consider the following questions:

1. According to Cannon, how many cents of every dollar spent on health care comes from the consumer?
2. Under the current employer-based health insurance system, how can consumers get more of a tax break, in Cannon's view?
3. Cannon says that opponents of the President's system will "scream that it would destroy employer-based health insurance." What does he think these opponents are really protesting?

In his State of the Union speech [in January 2007], President [George W.] Bush proposed steps to make health insurance more affordable by reducing taxes on health benefits for some workers and encouraging others to be more prudent health-care consumers. The changes would dramatically reduce the number of uninsured, allowing tens of millions of Americans to save thousands of dollars a year on insurance.

The president's plan would extend the tax exemption for health insurance to 18 million Americans who now buy coverage on their own, and to as many as 46 million more who have no insurance at all. It would let individuals deduct up to $7,500 per year in medical expenses, and families to deduct $15,000.

People without employer-provided coverage now pay for insurance with post-tax dollars. That means, in effect, that they pay taxes their neighbors don't.

Suppose Ms. Smith buys a $10,000 health plan for her family, while her neighbor Mr. Jones gets a $10,000 health plan from his employer. If, like 41 million other Americans,

Explaining the Tax Law

Under current health care laws, employees may exclude employer-paid coverage from their gross income as a fringe benefit under Section 106(a) of the Internal Revenue Code and employers may deduct amounts paid. However, those who pay for their own health insurance receive no deduction under Section 106 and receive only minor deductions throughout the Tax Code. These people must spend after-tax dollars on health insurance, which are deductible under Section 213 of the Internal Revenue Code "to the extent those expenses exceed 7.5% of adjusted gross income." This system strongly favors employer-provided health insurance through tax benefits creating an incentive to employers to provide additional compensation tax-free, while disfavoring individual-paid health insurance.

Dan Janes, The Journal of the Business Law Society,
February 16, 2007.

Ms. Smith's tax rate is 30 percent (including the 15 percent payroll tax for Social Security and Medicare), that means she pays almost $4,300 more.

(Yes, Mr. Jones' employer pays for the coverage and gets the tax break, but it's part of Jones' total compensation package—he gets the benefits, and would expect higher pay if he weren't getting it.)

President Bush plans to put an end to that. By giving Ms. Smith the same tax break as Mr. Jones, the president's proposal would save her $4,300 per year.

Encourage Responsibility

As it stands, the tax code also encourages Americans to consume more health care than they otherwise would. Employer-provided health insurance isn't taxed as income, so workers have an incentive to demand ever more generous health benefits. That's one reason why Americans are so heavily insured. For every dollar we spend on health care, on average we pay only 14 cents directly. (That makes us even more heavily insured than Canadians, who pay 15 cents on the dollar directly—and their socialized system is supposed to pay for everything.)

The incentive to demand more coverage often causes us to consume more health care than we need—which, in turn, drives health care prices and insurance premiums skyward.

The president's plan would encourage responsibility by limiting the amount of health insurance we can deduct from our taxes each year. The tax break for employer-provided health insurance is now unlimited, and workers can lower their taxes by demanding unnecessary coverage, which makes them less responsible as consumers.

According to White House estimates, the 20 percent of workers with the most expensive coverage would no longer be able to deduct their full health-insurance premiums. This would reduce the incentive for them to demand excessive coverage, which would help contain overall health care costs.

Giving Workers Choice and Control

Bush's proposal will be controversial. Opponents will scream that it would destroy employer-based health insurance. What those opponents actually mean, however, is that they don't think workers should be free to choose where they purchase their health insurance.

And the proposal isn't perfect. We should do more to give workers control of the money that employers spend on health benefits. Unless workers "own" those dollars, they might have to take a pay cut to exercise their new freedom to choose, which doesn't seem like freedom at all.

But such details shouldn't obscure the fact that this is a step in the right direction. Whatever else you may think about President Bush—and believe me, I have my share of gripes—he's the only prominent politician taking health care reform seriously. For that, he and his team deserve praise.

| *"The administration's plan does little to insure the uninsured, help the low income, or aid the less healthy."*

Tax Deductions on Health Benefits Will Not Help the Uninsured

Elise Gould

In the following viewpoint, Elise Gould argues that the George W. Bush administration's plan to offer tax incentives to prompt consumers to cheaper health insurance is wrongheaded. As Gould contends, the administration is hoping that if more people get health coverage through health savings accounts or similar plans instead of through expensive employer-based coverage, then the costs of health care will decline. Gould insists that those who might be swayed by these tax incentives are likely to be young, in good health, and low consumers of health services because they can afford to save up to meet any future crisis. The chronically ill or frailer members of society need more health care on a regular basis, and Gould fears they would be left in an eroding market of employer-based care, paying higher and higher premiums for the continual care they require. This would only exacerbate the health care crisis for those who are most dependent on care. Elise Gould is a member of the Economic Policy Institute, a non-profit think tank that researches economic policy. Gould's research work involves labor market trends and health-related economic issues.

As you read, consider the following questions:

1. Why does Gould state that it would be better policy to encourage rather than discourage employer-based health coverage?

2. Gould argues that low earners may not see any benefit from a tax exclusion credit because they would not make enough yearly income. How does she think this problem could be remedied?

3. What are some of the reasons Gould gives for why shifting the burden of acquiring health insurance to consumers is a bad idea?

President [George W.] Bush will [and did] set out in the [January 2007] State of the Union address a new health proposal that once again uses tax policy to encourage movement from employer-based health insurance system to one in which individuals buy health insurance on their own. Yet, the administration's plan does little to insure the uninsured, help the low income, or aid the less healthy.

The stated intent of the proposal is to equalize the individual and employer-based health insurance markets and create tax incentives for people to buy cheaper, less comprehensive plans so that consumers spend their health dollars more wisely. The current tax exclusion allows premiums from employer-based plans to be exempt from individual income tax and payroll taxes, which include Social Security and Medicare taxes. The Bush plan works like this: If workers purchase health insurance either through their employer or the individual market, a fixed amount is deducted from taxable income. The proposed tax deduction is $7,500 for individual plans and $15,000 for family plans. Thus, if you buy a single plan for $3,000, then you receive an additional tax deduction on the $4,500 you did not spend on health premiums.

Destabilizing Employer Risk Pools

Over time, this proposal will significantly erode the employer market. This is not particularly surprising as this administration has presided over a period of declining access to employer provided health insurance and has pushed and passed policies, such as Health Savings Accounts (HSAs), to advantage the individual market. However, it makes more sense to encourage the employer market because it produces larger risk pools, and keeps insurance more affordable for those who get sick and really need it. Employers provide a way to group people according to non-health characteristics, which makes them viable as insurance pools. A flat subsidy that encourages the purchase of the "leanest" (least comprehensive) insurance plan possible potentially siphons off the younger, healthier people into the individual market and destabilizes employer risk pools. The flat exclusion will likely affect few people in the beginning, but as health costs rise faster than the exclusion amount, it will cause further employer erosion in years to come.

Some people may be enticed by the new exclusion in the individual market to become insured. However, in the long-run, the erosion in the employer market may leave some of the neediest uninsurable in the individual market. Low-earners will not see many benefits from this plan for a simple reason—you need to make enough earnings for the tax exclusion to become valuable. If, for example, you spend much of the year uninsured because of unemployment, you almost surely will not have enough earnings to make any tax exclusion valuable. This problem could be fixed by making the flat exclusion

Tax Credit Winners and Losers

No serious health experts—and few American families—believe that a tax credit will help Americans get good health care coverage. Under a health care tax credit system, private insurance companies would still simply refuse to sell health insurance at an affordable price to those who really need it. Poor people cannot afford coverage—and, since the tax credits are not refundable, the poor will not be eligible. Middle-class families whose breadwinner is suddenly unemployed will likely have some family member with pre-existing conditions, which insurance companies use to deny coverage. Meanwhile, wealthy people . . . will buy whatever plan they were going to buy anyway and pocket the tax credit.

Isaiah J. Poole, TomPaine.com. February 7, 2007.
www.tompaine.com.

a "refundable" tax credit, like the Earned Income Tax Credit (EITC), which delivers benefits regardless of one's tax liability. Furthermore, cash-constrained workers cannot get the money now when they need to purchase the insurance. And, it is hard to imagine how the administration plans to handle the complex and costly nightmare of returning payroll taxes to all those non-filers.

An Incentive to Buy Less Comprehensive Insurance

Another problem with the Bush proposal is that it will create incentives to buy cheaper, less comprehensive insurance. Restrictions on the required coverage appear to be only minimal, giving individual insurance purchasers further inducement to buy high deductible health plans, particularly plans that qualify HSAs. All data suggest that these plans are unpopular. In fact, the proposal creates such a large incentive to buy less expensive policies that one wonders why the administration has chosen to continue the HSA preference for high deductible health plans.

The flat exclusion is supposed to tax 'Cadillac' health plans, allegedly because mostly high-income people have such extravagant health insurance. However, there is little evidence that the regressivity of current policy is due to a correlation between earnings and Cadillac health plans, rather, it stems from the simple fact that any tax exclusion necessarily provides benefits to those with high incomes (and hence high marginal tax rates). There is indeed little evidence to suggest that only high earners consume costly plans, and there are good reasons to think that they do not. Smaller firms employing one less-healthy employee or primarily older employees pay higher premiums. Even blue-collar workers who have successfully bargained for benefits often pay higher premiums. What is billed as progressive may not necessarily be so.

Many have decried the overall size of the tax expenditure resulting from current policy—the employer-exclusion is the single largest tax subsidy in the federal budget, more than double the size of the mortgage interest deduction. Moreover, the Bush proposal will increase the size of this expenditure, at least in the short-run. Support for this plan cannot be based on grounds of reducing the budget deficit.

Shifting Risk to Consumers

More than anything, the health policies introduced by the Bush administration [in January 2007] (and throughout the administration) are about shifting risk onto the individual. As the employer market erodes, more individuals must seek insurance on their own if they want any kind of health security. The individual market puts the onus on the individual to find and purchase health insurance, and there is no guarantee that the insurance they buy today will be available to them next year. Those unlucky enough to be unhealthy today or to get sick tomorrow will find it very difficult to find affordable insurance in the private market. At least the employer market promotes shared risk (or risk pooling) among individuals and families in firms and provides protection from financial loss when illness strikes. Risk pooling offers a way for individuals to share that risk. This year, your co-worker might need more health care and the next year, it might be you or your child that needs it.

To be clear, the current policy of exempting employer-based health insurance premiums from taxation is an expensive policy, benefiting only those with ties to the workplace. However, it does promote some measure of risk-pooling, which helps insurance markets function. Attacking this pooling without having a more comprehensive system in place to offer affordable, high-quality health insurance for those left without a pool is not a progressive endeavor.

| "Portable health insurance promises a continuing relationship with an insurer and, therefore, a continuing relationship with doctors and health facilities."

Health Insurance Should Be Portable

John Goodman

John C. Goodman is president of the National Center for Policy Analysis. He is the author of several books including Patient Power: Solving America's Health Care Crisis. *In the following viewpoint, Goodman argues that employer-based health insurance should be portable—that is, employees should be able to take it with them even if they switch jobs. Currently this is not possible because employers are required by law to buy group insurance for their employees if the insurance is to be untaxed (which is an incentive for employers). Goodman states that it would be better for the government to allow employers to buy untaxed individual insurance plans for their employees so that the workers could own the plans, transfer it from one workplace to another, and experience no disruption in health care when they change jobs.*

John Goodman, "Making Health Insurance Portable," *National Center for Policy Analysis*, January 30, 2006. Copyright © 2006 National Center for Policy Analysis. All rights reserved. Reproduced by permission. http://cdhc.ncpa.org.

As you read, consider the following questions:

1. What are some of the problems that Goodman says go along with the switching of health care plans from one workplace to another?

2. As Goodman explains, how do employers use health plans to discourage employees who are sick or have ill dependents from latching onto jobs just for the health benefits?

3. At what taxation threshold do people who buy their own health insurance receive a tax break, as Goodman relates?

One of the strange features of the U.S. health care system is that the health plan most of us have is not a plan that we chose; rather, it was selected by our employer. Even if we like our health plan, we could easily lose coverage because of the loss of a job, a change in employment or a decision by our employer. These problems affect all Americans, but lack of individually owned, personal and portable health insurance has its greatest impact on older workers, who are more likely to have health problems.

Lack of Continuity of Insurance

Virtually all employer health insurance contracts last only 12 months. At the end of the year, the employer—in search of ways to reduce costs—may choose a different health plan or cease providing health insurance altogether. Strangely, the only people with private health insurance guaranteed to last longer than one year are people who purchase insurance on their own.

Lack of Continuity of Care

Employer-sponsored health care largely evolved at a time when most health insurance was fee-for-service. Fee-for-service means an employee can see any doctor or enter any hospital and insurance paid all or most of the bills. As a result, a change of jobs usually did not cause undue disruption, provided that both the new and old employer had health insurance plans.

Things changed after the introduction of managed care. Today, as in the fee-for-service era, employees who switch jobs must also switch health plans. All too often, that means changing doctors as well, since each health plan tends to have its own network. For example, if an employee (or a member of the employee's family) has a health problem, there may be an interruption in the continuity of care. Additionally, different employer plans have different benefit packages. Thus, coverage for some services, like mental health, may be covered under one employer's plan but not under the next employer's plan.

These disruptions affect some families more than others. For people who are healthy, they may amount to minor inconveniences, but for others the problems can be severe. One study of chronically ill workers found that relying on one's employer for health coverage reduces job mobility by 40 percent compared to similar workers who obtain their health coverage elsewhere.

Perverse Incentives for Employers and Employees

Most employees view health insurance as a fringe benefit. When they enter the job market, they primarily search for employment opportunities that reward them for their skills and abilities. But a growing minority of workers approaches the job market very differently. These are individuals with a family member (often a spouse or child) who has very high health care costs. When these workers compare job opportunities, they are primarily comparing health plans. For them, health insurance is the main attraction, rather than the job or the pay.

Clearly it is not in the financial self interest of employers to attract workers whose primary motivation is to get their medical bills paid. So, to protect themselves from such potential hires, employers are increasingly altering their health plans to attract the healthy and avoid the sick. Having small copayments for routine office visits and higher deductibles for hospitalization is one technique. Having long waiting periods before employees become eligible for the company's health plan is another.

These reactions on the part of employers are rational responses to a labor market that increasingly is looking like a game of musical chairs. But what is good for the employer is not necessarily good for society as a whole.

Younger Spouses and Retirees on Medicare

The lack of individually owned, portable insurance is particularly burdensome for many women who are married to older men. When a husband retires and enrolls in Medicare, wives may be left without any coverage—and often at vulnerable times in their lives. At the same time, Medicare won't allow members to sign up underage spouses. Until the wife reaches 65 and can also enroll in Medicare, the couple will have to purchase her insurance with after-tax dollars. She'll also be at a time in her life when she's charged higher premiums for health insurance, since health risks tend to rise with age. And she'll pay even more (or possibly even be denied insurance altogether) if she already has an expensive health problem or is recovering from a disease such a breast cancer.

Federal Laws Designed to Encourage Portability Have Actually Outlawed It

Under the current system, employers cannot buy individually owned insurance for their employees. Specifically, lawyers interpret the Health Insurance Portability and Accountability Act of 1996 (HIPAA) to say that if employers purchase em-

> ## The Employer-Based Insurance System Is Antiquated
>
> Our system of tying health insurance to the workplace is becoming antiquated with a workforce that is increasingly independent and mobile. The Labor Department reports that four in ten Americans change jobs every year. With this kind of job mobility, it is extremely difficult to tie health insurance to the workplace and expect people to have continuity of coverage. People lose their jobs, and they lose their health insurance. We need a system that allows people to have health insurance that is portable; insurance that they can own and control; insurance that they, and not a politician or a human resources department, decide is right for them and their families.
>
> *Grace-Marie Turner, Heritage Lecture No. 1019, March 26, 2007.*
> *www.heritage.org.*

ployee health insurance with untaxed dollars, the insurance must be group insurance. A better alternative would allow employers to purchase individually owned, personal and portable insurance for their employees. Even though employers would pay some or all of the premiums, employees could take the insurance with them as they move from job to job.

Tax Penalties for Portable Insurance

Tax law is the main reason companies provide their workers with health insurance rather than pay higher wages with which employees could buy their own insurance.

People receiving employer-based health insurance enjoy an enormous tax advantage. Employer-paid premiums avoid federal, state and local income taxes, as well as the (FICA) payroll tax. By contrast, people who buy their own insurance get no tax break unless their medical costs exceed 7.5 percent of their adjusted gross income. Even then they get only a simple deduction and must itemize on their tax return. As a result, genuinely portable insurance is actually penalized under the tax law.

For a typical middle class family, government is effectively paying for half the cost of employer-provided health insurance. To see what this means, suppose that insurance for the family costs $6,000. If the insurance is purchased by an employer, it can be purchased with pretax dollars. This implies that the employee must produce and earn $6,000 that will be set aside as pretax payment for insurance rather than as taxable wages. However, if the insurance were to be purchased directly by the family, the employee must earn $12,000 in order to have enough left over after the payment of taxes to pay for the insurance. In terms of the amount of pretax income needed to purchase insurance, insurance purchased directly with after-tax dollars costs the family twice as much!

Creating Personal and Portable Health Insurance

Just because employers pay all or most of the premium does not mean that health insurance must necessarily be employer-specific. As an alternative, why can't employees enroll in health plans that meet their needs and stay in those plans as they travel from job to job? Personal and portable health insurance would solve many of these problems.

Employers should be able to buy personal and portable insurance for their employees. Even though employers initially would pay the premiums (as they do today), this insurance would be owned by the employees and would travel with them as they move through the labor market. Thus employees would get portable insurance (a characteristic of individual insurance), but they would get it at premiums that are closer to the norms of group insurance.

Although it is envisioned that employers initially will buy all their employees into the same health plan, with the passage of time, some of those employees will leave and go to work for other firms. Employers will also hire new employees who are members of other plans. And, in most cases, the employer's initial group of employees will be able to switch to other plans after a transition period. The typical employer, therefore, can eventually expect to have employees in different plans. Indeed, it is possible that every employee will be in a different plan.

Advantages of Portable Insurance

Portable health insurance promises a continuing relationship with an insurer and, therefore, a continuing relationship with doctors and health facilities. It also means that people can find a health plan they like and stay in it, without worrying whether they will be forced out of the plan by an employer's decision or by a change in employment.

For employers, portable health insurance means that small groups are no longer treated as a self-contained pool and rated each year based on changes in health status of their employees. Instead, their employees will be members of very large pools in which no one can be singled out because of a sudden large medical expense, and premium increases are the same for all. Under this system, employees can be in a plan of their own choosing and employers can limit their contribution to a fixed dollar amount. New hires will know how much the employer is going to contribute to health insurance, just as they know the amount of their salary. Because the employer's role is largely financial, in a real sense employers will get out of the "business" of health insurance.

> "The best way to enable individuals and families to buy, own, and keep health insurance from job to job ... is to transform the balkanized and dysfunctional state health insurance market into a single health insurance market."

A Health Insurance Exchange Will Make Health Care More Affordable

Robert E. Moffit

In the following viewpoint, Robert E. Moffit states that the U.S. tax code penalizes people who want to buy individual health care plans by not affording them the tax breaks provided employer-based coverage. Since Moffit maintains that Congress will not likely change the tax code soon, he supports the creation of state health insurance exchanges that would act as single marketplaces (similar to stock exchanges) in which individual health plans could vie for a share of the consumer base. As Moffit envisions, employers would make tax-free contributions to the exchange to pay for the plans that their employees select. The exchange would allow consumers to maintain plans if they switch

Robert E. Moffit, "The Rationale for a Statewide Health Insurance Exchange," *Heritage Foundation WebMemo*, October 5, 2006. © 2007 The Heritage Foundation. Reproduced by permission. www.heritage.org.

*jobs, and it would reduce the costs of individual plans by provid-
ing the tax breaks currently associated with employer-based
group insurance. Robert E. Moffit is the director of the Center for
Health Policy Studies at the Heritage Foundation, a public policy
research institution that values freedom, opportunity, and pros-
perity.*

As you read, consider the following questions:

1. In Moffit's view, what bold steps could Congress take to
   improve the health care market in a manner that would
   be even better than the creation of health insurance exchanges?
2. What are the "major benefits" of health insurance exchanges for employers, according to Moffit?
3. As Moffit states, who should ideally be able to acquire
   health insurance through a state exchange?

U. S. health insurance markets are governed by a complex
system of state and federal laws and regulations, many
of which are outdated and counter-productive. The most important of these laws is the federal tax code. Americans get
unlimited federal tax breaks for the purchase of health insurance if they receive that coverage through their workplace.
Outside of the workplace, however, they almost always pay for
coverage with after-tax dollars. Statewide health insurance exchanges are a solution to this inefficient inconsistency, giving
individuals and families the opportunity to secure the health
plans of their choice without losing tax benefits.

The Federal Tax Code Distorts
Insurance Markets

The federal tax code profoundly distorts health insurance
markets. By law, Congress ties the enormous tax benefits of
health insurance almost exclusively to the place of work. Workers who buy health coverage outside of the employer-based

system often have to cope not only with high administrative costs and inflexible government mandates, but also with the loss of federal and state tax breaks. The loss of these tax breaks could add 40 to 50 percent to the cost of a policy purchased through the place of work.

Employers do not own auto, life, homeowners', or property and casualty insurance policies on behalf of their employees. Indeed, most Americans would find such arrangements strange. But in contrast to every other type of insurance in the private market, health insurance in the United States sticks to the job, not the person. Employers own health insurance policies; individuals and families do not.

The current tax law also directly affects coverage. Recent empirical data shows that among the total number of the uninsured, the proportion of long-term uninsured is small—only slightly more than one out of ten over a four-year period. The overwhelming majority of the uninsured are in and out of coverage, usually due to changes in their job situation. They had access to insurance but lost it. Without personal ownership of health insurance policies, there is not any real portability in coverage. The problem is not simply access to health insurance coverage; it is also keeping that coverage. The right policy, then, would have health insurance stick to the person, not the job.

Congressional Inaction

Congress could simply change the federal tax code to give individuals and families tax relief for the purchase of health insurance regardless of where they work so that they can buy and own the coverage they want at competitive prices. In other words, by changing the tax code, Congress could take a dramatic step to creating a real, consumer-driven health insurance market. Going even further, if Congress allowed interstate commerce in health insurance—letting individuals and families to buy coverage across state lines from any state in the United States—it would create a single national market for insurance coverage. In this large market, with large health insurance pools, individuals and families would own and control their own health insurance. These reforms would create a robust system of consumer choice and competition.

A State Exchange Would Create a Unified Marketplace

Short of congressional action to reform the tax code, the burden to improve health coverage rests with state officials. The best way to enable individuals and families to buy, own, and keep health insurance from job to job—without losing the tax advantages of the employment-based coverage—is to transform the balkanized and dysfunctional state health insurance market into a single health insurance market. This new market would function well for all sorts off individuals and small businesses, not just workers employed by large companies.

A sound legal framework is necessary to secure fully functioning and efficient markets. Current law governing health insurance in many states does not work well to control costs or to expand personal access to coverage. Accordingly, state officials who are serious about creating new, consumer-based systems need to create a new legal framework for health insurance.

The best option is a health insurance market exchange. A properly designed health insurance exchange would function as a single market for all kinds of health insurance plans, including traditional insurance plans, health maintenance organizations, health savings accounts, and other new coverage options that might emerge in response to consumer demand. In principle, it would function like a stock exchange, which is a single market for all varieties of stocks and reduces the costs of buying, selling, and trading stocks. For the same reasons, other types of market transactions are also centralized, such as farmers' markets, single locations where shoppers can purchase a variety of fresh fruits and vegetables, and Carmax, where consumers can choose from among all kinds of makes and models of automobiles.

In the case of a statewide health insurance exchange, employers would designate the health insurance exchange itself as their "plan" for the purpose of the federal and state tax codes. Thus all defined contributions would be tax free, just as they would be for conventional employer-based health insurance. The major benefits of this arrangement for employers, particularly small employers, are a reduction in administrative costs and paperwork and the ability to make defined contributions to their employees' preferred plans.

As a vehicle for a defined-contribution approach to health care financing, an exchange would expand coverage and choice. Rather than have to decide whether to pay for full coverage or not, employers could make defined contributions of any size to the exchange. Moreover, employers could also enable employees, including those working part-time and on contract, to buy health insurance with pre-tax dollars. Under a Section 125 plan, any premium payments made by workers, even part-time workers or contract employees, would be 100 percent tax-free. This is especially important for workers in firms that require them to pay part of the health insurance premium. Employees, not employers, would buy the health care coverage with *pre-tax* dollars, would own their own health plans, and would take them from job to job without the loss of the generous tax benefits of conventional employer-based coverage. This is a revolutionary change in the health insurance market.

Unlike other state-based initiatives, the creation of a statewide health insurance exchange would not violate the Employee Retirement Income Security Act of 1974 (ERISA). This approach complies with ERISA because employer participation in an exchange is *voluntary*—though, given the benefits of an exchange, few small businesses would turn down the

Support for Massachusetts' Health Insurance Exchange Experiment

[A State health insurance] exchange offers numerous advantages. For example, a two-earner couple could combine contributions from their respective employers to buy and keep the plan they want, instead of being forced to choose one employer's plan while forgoing the subsidy offered by the other employer. Similarly, a worker with two part-time jobs could combine prorated contributions from each employer to buy coverage, while the government would have a single place to send subsidies for those who need extra help.

In short, the exchange is designed to work around the limitations of current federal law to achieve, in a single state, the basic objectives of conservative health reform—consumer choice of plans, true coverage portability, and the functional equivalent of individual health-insurance tax credits to help pay for coverage.

Edmund F. Haislmaier, National Review
Online, *January 27, 2006.*

option. An exchange can be designed within the existing framework of other federal insurance laws, including the Consolidated Omnibus Budget Reconciliation Act (COBRA) and the Health Insurance Portability and Accountability Act (HIPAA).

A Non-Regulatory Body

A health insurance exchange could be the basis of a new legal framework for health insurance at the state level. It could replace much of the existing state law, which creates separate individual and small group markets and governs balkanized and overregulated state health insurance markets. Ideally, an exchange should be open to all state residents and all interested employers, regardless of the size of the firm, who want to arrange health insurance through the exchange.

The specific functions of an exchange would be mechanical, not regulatory. An exchange should not license or standardize health plans or impose underwriting rules or benefit mandates. The focus should be on processing paperwork—mostly processing employer and employee contributions or independent premium payments—and administering enrollment and coverage selection through an annual open season, it should function just like the human resources department of a very large employer. An exchange could also be a mechanism for the administration of government subsidies for low-income persons, if state officials wanted to extend that help. Similarly, it could be a mechanism for the administration of federal health care tax credits for individuals and families, if Congress should ever decide to enact individual tax relief for health care and help individuals and families without employer-based coverage.

An exchange should be administered by a nongovernmental entity operating under a special state government charter. Irrespective of the organizational structure, the functions of an exchange could be contracted out to private entities or private third-party administrators. From the perspective of health policy, the issue of governance is of secondary importance.

A Temporary Solution

State-level health insurance exchanges would increase health insurance coverage, significantly lower prices in the individual coverage market, give individuals and families access to more choice, allow coverage portability, and increase employers' flexibility in offering health benefits.

Congress should reform the tax treatment of health insurance. But short of congressional action to rectify the inequities of the federal tax code, a health insurance exchange is the best way for individuals and families to secure personal and portable health insurance without incurring heavy tax penalties.

Periodical Bibliography

The following articles have been selected to supplement the diverse views presented in this chapter.

America	"Bush's Health Care Plan Seen as Inadequate," Feburary 20, 2006.
Steve Chapman	"Bush's Health Plan Has Modesty Among Its Virtues," *Chicago Tribune*, January 28, 2007.
Clive Crook	"A Glimmer of Purpose in the Pantomime," *National Journal*, January 27, 2007.
Christopher Farrell	"Health Care You Control," *Business Week*, May 28, 2007.
Stephen Gorin	"The Trouble with Health Savings Accounts: A Social Work Perspective," *Health & Social Work*, November 2006.
Janice A. Hauge	"Contradictory Incentives in the Medicare+Choice Medical Savings Account Program," *CATO Journal*, Winter 2006.
Hendrik Hertzberg	"Consumption," *New Yorker*, April 17, 2006.
Jennifer Lubell	"Hospital Stays of Uninsured Stable: AHRQ," *Modern Healthcare*, June 5, 2006.
Jennifer Lubell and Jessica Zigmond	"Rob Hospitals to Pay Poor," *Modern Health-care*, January 29, 2007.
Pat Mail	"Universal Health Care: Creating a System That Works for All," *Nation's Health*, October 2006.
Laura Meckler	"How Plans to Expand Health Coverage Could Affect Insured," *Wall Street Journal*, February 6, 2007.
Jane Bryant Quinn and Temma Ehrenfeld	"Health Care's New Lottery," *Newsweek*, February 27, 2006.
Jan M. Rosen	"Health Insurance and Other Benefits: A Primer," *New York Times*, May 16, 2007.

OPPOSING
VIEWPOINTS®
SERIES

CHAPTER 4

How Should State Health Care Programs Be Altered?

Chapter Preface

In April 2006 the legislature of Massachusetts almost unanimously passed a bill to provide near-universal coverage for all the state's residents. Governor Mitt Romney was a key architect and staunch supporter of the bill, after coming to the realization: "People who don't have insurance nonetheless receive health care. And it's expensive." Romney figured, "We're spending a billion dollars giving health care to people who don't have insurance. And my question was: Could we take that billion dollars and help the poor purchase insurance? Let them pay what they can afford. We'll subsidize what they can't." The governor and the legislature were also prompted to take action once the federal government threatened to cut Medicaid funds, almost guaranteeing that more residents would join the ranks of the uninsured.

The legislation insists that nearly all businesses provide health insurance coverage of some kind for their workers or incur significant fines. The state intends to offer incentives to insurers to work with smaller companies and provide basic coverage plans at reduced rates. In addition, individuals who do not receive employer-based insurance but can afford private plans must do so or also face income tax penalties. Those at the bottom rung of the economic ladder can pay relatively meager sums to purchase a state-subsidized plan. State authorities expect the plan to cover 95 percent of the state's uninsured population within a three-year period.

Critics of the Massachusetts plan claim that some of the money earmarked for aid will have to fund a new bureaucracy that will oversee the program and administer subsidies. Sally Pipes, the president of the Pacific Research Institute, says that in particular the monitoring of all those who are compelled to buy insurance "will be expensive to enforce." Pipes and others argue that once premiums begin to rise (because the state has no power over the insurers or their policies), the legislature will have to step in to regulate the system, which in turn will lead to government-controlled health care.

Wary of this outcome but still interested in a plan that does not raise state taxes, other state governments are watching Massachusetts's experiment. In the following chapter, various commentators examine state-based programs that provide health benefits to low-income and vulnerable populations. Chief among the issues under debate are whether these programs are meeting the needs of the uninsured or whether the programs have been so abused as to make their expenses unjustified, thus paving the way for more revolutionary solutions such as the Massachusetts plan.

"I would not be alive to type this without Medicaid."

Medicaid Funds Should Not Be Cut

Nick Dupree

Nick Dupree, a disability rights activist, argues in the following viewpoint that the George W. Bush administration's cuts to Medicaid—the state administered health insurance that is available to qualifying individuals because of low income, disability, age, or other determining factor—are detrimental. Dupree attests that while the government slashes funds to balance budgets, the people who are in the most need of Medicaid funds are facing the consequences. Many cannot afford private insurance, and Dupree asserts that some of his friends have even died when specific Medicaid benefits were withdrawn.

As you read, consider the following questions:

1. According to Dupree, with what had President Bush proposed to replace Medicaid early in his term?
2. What does Dupree say are the motivating philosophies behind the Republican party's platform to cut Medicaid?

Nick Dupree, "Vigorously Insisting on a More Perfect Union: Fighting Cuts, Demanding Universal Health Care," *Nick Dupree Blogs for Social Justice*, February 15, 2007. Reproduced by permission of the author. http://nickdupree.blogspot.com.

3. What example does Dupree use to show that Medicaid
   has had a positive impact on saving people's lives?

It has almost become a spring ritual for me. President
[George W.] Bush submits a new budget to Congress, un-
abashedly filled with loathsome cuts to the lifeline of the poor
and disabled (Medicaid) to finance more tax rebates for billionaires and Exxon. I then write a column in the college
newspaper challenging the country's backwards priorities, or,
since '05, I blog about here. But it is every year, it never fails,
for six years now. Each year I take up my quixotic sword and
crusade against the dragons of rightist immorality, and I'm
sick of it, fed up with the harsh toll paid by the disabled minority in increased suffering and death. . . .

Impact of Budget Cuts

Initially Bush proposed to *end the Medicaid program* in favor
of no-strings-attached block grants to the states that would be
severely capped and unchangeable if your state has increased
needs. This was such a horrible idea and would throw states
with already broken and neglected Medicaid systems into such
a terrible tailspin of public health and economic crisis, that
the (then majority Republican) National Governor's Association, backed by lots of advocacy from disabilities groups,
made Bush drop the plan.

However, deep, sweeping cuts have been proposed by President Bush every year he's been employed here. Usually the Republican Congress would pare down the cuts from devastating
to merely horrible before sending them to the president's desk
to be signed into law, so while our health care system hasn't
collapsed totally due to cuts, it has been hurt dearly.

Americans largely like to pretend budgetary changes such
as these have no real effect on their lives. The administration
is arguing that their plan to slash $70 billion from Medicare
and Medicaid won't dent the growth of the program OVER-
ALL, but tell that to the disabled guy who was just told wait

ing lists for medical assistance are now extended indefinitely due to the cuts to the already-neglected system. Tell that to the paraplegic guy who was dumped out onto the street on Skid Row with a broken colostomy bag last week by a Hollywood Presbyterian Medical Center van, leaving him to crawl on the sidewalk with nothing but a hospital gown and his own feces. There is inadequate funding all over. We need huge increases if we are to address the massive unmet needs that exist and achieve something of a just society.

People Depend on Medicaid

For those with severe disabilities dependent on Medicaid, the Republican cuts from 1995–2007 have had horrible consequences. I've had to fight like hell to survive. In 1996 in Alabama, Medicaid started gutting EPSDT [Early and Periodic Screening, Diagnostic, and Treatment service] (the federally-mandated program providing nursing care for those in need) and sending out termination notices to families in the mail. Then in 1999–2001 we had more aggressive cuts. They changed the rules so it's only a temporary program to train caregivers to stay with their child 24/7, and they keep repeating that it is not the government's role to "babysit" your child at all (even if your child is on life support and routinely coding). And now it is 2007 and Alabama barely funds it at all. We've almost been rolled back into the 1970s level. I've had friends die. I'm sick of tolerating this evil like it is a valid policy position. It is in no way valid nor deserving of our deference and patience. It is nothing but immoral.

Let's go deeper. What are the motivating factors behind loathsome public policy of this nature? From all I've learned, and what is printed openly in the Republican party platform, the ideologies are basically:

1) the private sector is always more efficient and effective than government, therefore we should cut back Medicaid as much as possible so the free market can create innovative solutions.

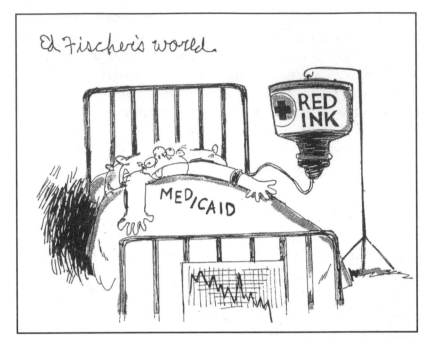

"Medicaid Patient Being Killed with Red Ink," cartoon by Ed Fischer. Cartoon Stock.com.

2) "I don't want to pay for you." Taxation is always bad, therefore we should cut back Medicaid as much as possible so we'll have less to pay for.

Both of these are wrong and destructive, yet are widely echoed in America in words and in voting patterns.

I have seen too much suffering and death because of inadequate supports and invisible safety nets, and I am frakking traumatized that people are still pushing this destructive right-wing mythology that if we chip away at government funding even further, that this will magically increase services. It has been tried for years and has failed every time.

How Medicaid Helps

Medicaid saves lives. Since introducing Medicaid and other programs in the '60s, infant mortality in America has dropped by 1/3 (the free market previously let those babies die). Medicaid keeps me alive. I would not be alive to type this without Medicaid. We've had over a decade of budget cuts pushed by the aforementioned misconceptions, and now Alabama has almost no Medicaid at all; it has been cut back to barely existing. Where are all these wonderful private systems aiding people with disabilities? Nowhere to be found. What fills the gap? Nothing does. There is no free market incentive to help people with disabilities here. People fall through the cracks and die over and over and over and over. I'm beyond fury and disgust at what Alabama has done.

Yet we can still entertain the fantasy that if government just goes away, the market will devise a better system? I've even seen some people with disabilities writing, "yes, I don't mind if they cut Medicaid 'vote GOP'" shortsightedly believing it won't effect them (evidently it's okay to hurt someone else as long as it isn't you) These ideas should be long-since discredited and abandoned as purely destructive to our basic survival.

If you gut government funding and leave people with disabilities to the free market jungle, they are devalued and thrown aside

The Market Is Not Designed to Help People

I am arguing the fundamental truth that reducing funding for people with disabilities does not magically increase funding for people with disabilities. I am arguing the fundamental truth that very few of the severely disabled would ever survive without help, our needs are expensive, and I don't see the free market ever giving us services for free (the market is wonderful for many things like efficiently meeting demand for widgets, but keeping us alive isn't one of them). Therefore, we need government funding, and (if this is properly prioritized) substantially MORE government funding, not less.

In a perfect world (known in Judaism as the Messianic Age) all health care would be free. It would be patently obvious to everyone that this immoral system that makes sick people fork over all their assets or die, is to be abandoned!

The rift between me and the Republicans in power is I am trying to build a more perfect union NOW with free health care for everyone, and they are fighting it tooth and nail, in an idolatrous mindset against every major religious text that makes money and serving money the center, not mitzvos (commandments/good deeds).

My politics are an essential mandate stemming from the basic moral and spiritual system I have always had. Because the national Republican platform embraces the despicable policy of slashing aid for the poor and disabled (those who need it most) and giving the money in huge tax cuts to those who need it least (billionaires), because for three decades they have aggressively pushed gigantic rebates for oil corporations (that already have bigger profits than the GDPs [gross domestic products] of *most countries*) as of far greater importance than funding health care and reducing our infant mortality (which is still bad and behind Cuba's) and because of these policy differences. I doubt I will ever ever ever ever support a Republican for president. Democrats, while chock-full of their own problems, have opposed cutting health care every time. It is from this framework that I will be assessing candidates for president and their health care plans.

And I'll continue opposing every attempt to cut health care.

"In states that have imposed cost increases ... , [Medicaid] enrollments
have declined steeply, and signs have
emerged that poor people are limiting
their usage of services."

Medicaid Cost Sharing Is Hurting the Poor

Michelle Chen

Michelle Chen was a staff reporter for The NewStandard, *a
now-defunct online newspaper. In the following viewpoint, Chen
contends that the decision of some states to raise Medicaid co-
payments and premiums is bad policy. Chen states that these
"cost sharing" initiatives are nothing more than a way to shift
the burden of medical care onto those who can least afford it.
Medicaid is designed to help low-income individuals, the elderly,
children, and other disadvantaged groups, and Chen warns that
these populations are being forced to drop their coverage or seek
services less often as the price of public aid rises.*

As you read, consider the following questions:

1. About how many people are served by Medicaid, as
   Chen states?

2. According to the Center on Budget and Policy Priorities, as reported by Chen, by what percentage has the payment for prescription drugs risen for disabled and non-disabled Medicaid beneficiaries between 1997 and 2002?

3. As Chen claims, what percentage of those who lost Medicaid coverage in Oregon failed to find other medical insurance?

As a rollback on federal Medicaid funding crystallizes in Congress [in 2005] with a $10 billion budget cut, analysts predict that tightening fiscal pressures on state health systems will spur governments to shift a greater share of the healthcare burden onto economically disadvantaged populations.

Health policy experts at the progressive Washington think tank Center on Budget and Policy Priorities and the Kaiser Family Foundation, a healthcare research organization, have released new reports documenting the impact of so-called "cost-sharing" initiatives—such as increased co-payments for services and higher premiums—imposed on Medicaid recipients in various states.

The research indicates that policies to increase the amount people must pay for government-subsidized healthcare could have a dramatic effect not only on access to services in general, but on the health of the poorest and most vulnerable groups—people who typically depend on the public safety net to meet their medical needs. In states that have imposed cost increases and similar impediments to services, enrollments have declined steeply, and signs have emerged that poor people are limiting their usage of services and seeing their health deteriorate as a result.

A Focus on Money, Not Public Aid

Presenting recent research findings at a press conference [on May 31, 2005], Judy Feder, dean of Georgetown University's Public Policy Institute, remarked that attempts to cut the costs of Medicaid, at both federal and state levels, focused exclusively on budgetary concerns without addressing deeper issues that prevent people from obtaining necessary care. "The real problem the nation faces is not with the Medicaid program. It's ... the low incomes of people on Medicaid, and the high costs of medical care."

Medicaid is the country's most comprehensive public health program, serving 38 million people, including low-income adults, children and seniors. Jointly funded and administered by state and federal governments, individual states' programs have in recent years expanded or retracted services and enrollment in response to economic and budgetary fluctuations.

Federal mandates for the Medicaid program limit the contributions states can require from beneficiaries in the form of co-payments and premiums. But since the 1990s, many states have obtained special federal waivers that enable them to adjust their cost-sharing plans or eligibility rules in response to local circumstances, such as an initiative to expand coverage to certain groups or a state budget crunch.

Kaiser Foundation researchers reported that state governments have promoted cost-sharing initiatives as a way to increase what they call "personal responsibility" and flexibility among healthcare recipients. Last year, twenty states raised medical co-payments for beneficiaries, and nine states are slated to do so during 2005.

Cost Sharing Means More Out-of-Pocket Expense

Recent research suggests that the net effects of the increased medical payments have been a shrinkage in benefits and services available to low-income people, a heavier economic burden on individuals and families, and the indirect consequence of people being deterred from accessing care, sometimes avoiding treatment until an emergency situation.

An analysis of national Medicaid data from 1997 to 2002 by the Center on Budget and Policy Priorities found that for adults living in poverty who are not elderly or disabled, out-of-pocket medical costs rose by an average of over 9 percent a year—double the rate of income growth. By contrast, middle-income, privately insured adults saw their out-of-pocket expenses grow by only 6 percent.

Among both disabled and non-disabled adult beneficiaries, direct payments for prescription drugs jumped by roughly 15 percent annually, and out-of-pocket Medicaid costs in general have consumed a growing portion of their household income.

According to the Kaiser Foundation report, when Rhode Island enacted monthly premium rates of $43 to $58 for people with incomes above one-and-a-half times the poverty line, within three months, 20 percent of enrolled households were forced out of the program for failure to pay. In a follow-up survey, half of the disenrolled families said the higher premiums had forced them to drop out of the program.

In Maryland's State Child Health Insurance Program, a Medicaid-related healthcare plan offered to Medicaid-ineligible children, the State-imposed premiums of $37 per month for children living at around double the poverty level. Nearly 30 percent of children affected by the policy fell off the rolls, and 20 percent of surveyed disenrolled families cited the premium as a factor in pulling their children out of the program, which later prompted the government to rescind the policy.

Oregon's Severe Medicaid Policy

Some of the most drastic impacts of increasing payments for Medicaid services have been demonstrated in Oregon, where the government, facing a budget crisis in 2003, combined increased program costs with stricter enrollment rules. Legislators installed a two-tier system of coverage that imposed new

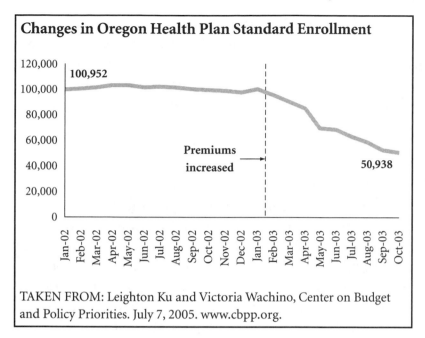

Changes in Oregon Health Plan Standard Enrollment

TAKEN FROM: Leighton Ku and Victoria Wachino, Center on Budget and Policy Priorities. July 7, 2005. www.cbpp.org.

premiums and co-payments on the "non-mandatory" Medicaid population—adults living below the poverty line who would not otherwise qualify for Medicaid under the more limited federal eligibility statutes.

Under the new policy, a beneficiary who missed a payment would be automatically dropped from coverage, even in cases of financial emergency or if the person had zero income. After the plan took effect in early 2003, enrollment plummeted from nearly 90,000 to less than 50,000, and is now approaching a state-mandated cap of 24,000.

New research sheds light on how the costs of healthcare are often "shared" by the poor population in the form of poorer health and financial insecurity. According to survey data, nearly 70 percent of those who lost coverage in Oregon as a result of the Medicaid restructuring failed to find another source of insurance.

Compared to those who stayed on Medicaid, people who lost coverage were four times more likely to rely on emergency rooms served as the main source of medical care. Among extremely poor, chronically ill respondents, living below 10 percent of the poverty line, half of the disenrolled population reported a recent visit to the emergency room, compared with one-third of those who remained in the program.

According to one Oregon healthcare advocate, service providers have reported that the recent Medicaid policy changes, in addition to reducing enrollment, have also deterred people even from public facilities that accept patients regardless of ability to pay. As many face a combination of prohibitive costs, tighter enrollment rules, and limited knowledge about their eligibility for healthcare, "There's been a certain proportion. . . who stop coming in and likely go into emergency rooms," said Laura Sisulak, director of policy of the Oregon Primary Care Association, an organization representing the state's public healthcare centers and clinics.

Sisulak also noted that the public healthcare system has been forced to absorb the growth in the uninsured population since the new Medicaid rules took effect. Clinics have responded to budgetary strains by reducing staff or operating hours, she said.

The Costs Do Not Go Away

A study by researchers at the Oregon Health & Science University revealed that the enactment of cost-sharing initiatives was followed by a substantial increase in emergency room visits by the uninsured, including people with mental health and substance abuse problems, who are frequently unable to obtain treatment by other means.

"Every part of the healthcare system impacts the other," Sisulak told *The NewStandard*. So, while a policy may save money in one program, ultimately "costs don't go away."

Healthcare advocates argue that when governments cut expenditures by raising rates for beneficiaries, the sickest and the poorest tend to feel the pinch. Speaking at the press conference, Leighton Ku, a health policy fellow with the Center on Budget and Policy Priorities, explained, "The greater the savings you try to incur ... the more risks that you're creating, and the more problems that you're creating for low-income beneficiaries."

Though state governments have touted cost-sharing programs as a way to more evenly distribute both the costs and benefits of Medicaid, critics see them as a calculated shift of budgetary burdens from government coffers to the pockets of those with the least.

"Proposals to increase cost-sharing or premium payments for Medicaid eligibles," said Feder, "should be recognized as what they are: proposals to increase barriers to access to care."

*"Why [should] Medicaid ... be used as
a kind of inheritance insurance for
middle-class baby-boomer heirs?"*

Medicaid Is Becoming
Public Welfare

Stephen A. Moses

*In the following viewpoint, Stephen A. Moses, the president of
the Center for Long Term Care Reform in Seattle, Washington,
argues that loopholes in the Medicaid system allow many wealthy
seniors to claim benefits. Moses maintains that otherwise-
ineligible seniors are able to hide their money in exempt accounts and distribute their assets to their children and then
claim impoverishment in order to meet Medicaid requirements.
Although Moses says that Congress is taking action to close the
loopholes, they face stiff resistance from organizations such as the
American Association of Retired Persons (AARP) that insist that
tightening requirements will reduce access to those in need.*

As you read, consider the following questions:

1. How much combined home equity do American seniors
   possess, according to Moses?

2. As Moses states, when did Congress criminalize "Medicaid planning"? What happened to that measure?

3. What tactics has the AARP utilized to fight changes to Medicaid, as Moses reports?

With expenditures topping $300 billion and rising 8% annually, Medicaid is a huge entitlement—larger even than Medicare. State governors in particular are howling that their share of the overall costs—43%—are burning through state budgets uncontrollably. As Virginia's Mark Warner put it, "We are on the road to a meltdown."

Now [in late 2005], as the first session of the 109th Congress winds down, House and Senate members are attempting to hash out a compromise in conference that could provide some overall budget relief. The spoiler is AARP [American Association of Retired Persons], which is dispensing clouds of self-serving rhetoric while attempting to divert the program's scarce resources to the senior lobby's more affluent members. What's going on?

Most people think of Medicaid as the health-care payer of last resort for poor women and children. But long-term care is Medicaid's biggest single cost—and many recipients of this largesse are anything but poor. One reason is that, for purposes of Medicaid nursing home eligibility, people are allowed to retain unlimited income as long as their medical expenses—including long-term care—are high enough. Another big reason is that they can also keep unlimited assets in the form of home equity, a business or other kinds of wealth.

In theory, once they die the government could recover Medicaid costs from their estates. In practice, most of this wealth disappears, often in gifts to family members.

Loopholes to Protect Those with Assets

Consider home equity, seniors' largest asset. According to the National Council on the Aging, 81% of America's 13.2 million householders aged 62 and over own their own homes, and

74% own their homes free and clear. Altogether, seniors possess nearly $2 trillion worth of home equity. Yet, by the time they apply for Medicaid, few own their homes. Are they giving the homes away to their grown-up children or other relatives? Such a transfer of assets carries no legal penalty as long as it is done at least three years and a day before applying for Medicaid.

That's just one of hundreds of eligibility "loopholes" that allow individuals, especially those advised by Medicaid planning attorneys, to qualify for Medicaid long-term care benefits without spending down their own wealth for care. If you doubt this, try an Internet search for "Medicaid planning" and read some of the sales pitches on the more than six million hits. You'll learn how to purchase noncountable assets, buy and give away a string of luxury cars without penalty, hide wealth in exempt annuities, sell your ailing parent a "life-care contract," even buy a farm or business—all for the express purpose of "impoverishing" yourself or a loved one artificially and qualifying for Medicaid long-term care benefits.

Ten Congresses and four presidents have tried to stop these legal scams. They've closed loopholes, discouraged Medicaid qualifying trusts, made recovery from recipients' estates mandatory, and offered tax incentives to encourage private insurance. They even criminalized Medicaid planning in 1996, only to be accused of "throwing granny in jail." When they repealed that measure and replaced it a year later with another to "throw granny's lawyer in jail," the law was deemed unconstitutional.

Congress is trying Medicaid reform once again. The House of Representatives . . . passed legislation to curtail a few of the most egregious abuses. It would move the look-back period for asset transfers from three to five years, eliminate Medicaid planners' favorite "half-a-loaf" giveaway strategy, and cap exempt home equity at $750,000. Even if these measures move out of the conference committee with the Senate and become

---

Reverse Mortgages Can Help Pay Medical Expenses

This is another tool that could help prevent individuals with considerable assets from depending upon Medicaid. According to the U.S. Census Bureau, 81 percent of seniors own their homes and 73 percent own them free and clear. This represents $1.9 trillion in untapped home equity that is currently exempted from Medicaid's eligibility calculations. According to the National Council on Aging, 48 percent of America's 13.2 million households age 62 and older could get $72,128 on average from reverse mortgages, and "in total, an estimated $953 billion could be available from reverse mortgages for immediate long-term care needs and to promote aging in place."

National Governors Association, "Medicaid Reform: A Preliminary Report," June 15, 2005.

---

law [they did in early 2006] elderly Americans could still give away $10 million (actually unlimited assets) without penalty five years and one day before applying for Medicaid. They, could still retain a home worth three-quarters of a million dollars while getting taxpayers to pick up the costs of their long-term care.

AARP Backlash

AARP has nevertheless gone ballistic, claiming that the House reforms "seriously threaten the ability of millions of Americans to get needed long-term care services" and "will deny millions of older and disabled Americans the long-term care services they, need and leave them vulnerable to substandard care." They've targeted members of Congress with advertisements in their hometown papers attacking the House's efforts to curtail Medicaid abuse; they've run radio and TV spots, and full-page ads appear in Capitol Hill papers almost daily. House staffers report that scared and angry AARP members have been deluging members' offices with calls and letters parroting AARP's distortions and hyperbole.

AARP's position and tactics are wrong, hurtful and dangerous. Preventing asset giveaways to qualify for public assistance does not threaten one's access to quality long-term care: If people keep their wealth instead of giving it away, they will command red-carpet access to top-quality care in the private market instead of becoming dependent on Medicaid's low-cost nursing home care of highly questionable quality.

Denying public welfare to people with three-quarters of a million dollars in home equity does not reduce their access to care. With a reverse mortgage, such people can tap their home equity to pay for long-term care, or indeed to pay for private long-term care insurance. As private payers, such people will have better access to a wider range of higher quality long-term care services than they would have as Medicaid dependents.

Abusing the System

The more fundamental questions to ask are why Medicaid should be used as a kind of inheritance insurance for middle-class baby-boomer heirs—and how this practice protects Americans most in need? AARP's resistance to Medicaid reform anesthetizes boomers to the risk and cost of long-term care at the very time in their lives when they should be saving, investing and insuring against such risks. It lines their pockets now at the expense of taxpayers, to the detriment of the poor, and with a huge risk to Medicaid's solvency.

Boil it all down and you're left with only one conclusion. Faced with the choice of supporting the use of Medicaid for people genuinely in need, or grabbing what it can for its well-heeled members and their heirs, AARP took the low road.

> "There are still some 9 million children living in the United States who lack coverage for basic health care."

The State Children's Health Insurance Program Should Be Expanded

Partnership for Medicaid

The Partnership for Medicaid is a nonpartisan, nationwide effort by safety net providers and other key organizations to preserve and improve the Medicaid program. Its membership includes such organizations as the American College of Physicians, the American Academy of Pediatrics, and the AFL-CIO. In the following viewpoint, the Partnership for Medicaid presents its case for expanding the State Children's Health Insurance Program (SCHIP) to two ranking members of the U.S House Committee on Energy and Commerce. The partnership argues that many underprivileged children rely on SCHIP programs but that more who deserve coverage are yet to be served. The partnership urges that SCHIP incorporate expanded benefits (such as dental and mental health insurance) and do away with restrictions on enrollment and documentation processes.

As you read, consider the following questions:

1. How much more was slated to fund SCHIP for the 2007 congressional budget, as the partnership reports?
2. What is "Express Lane" enrollment, and how would it help children who are eligible for SCHIP benefits, according to the partnership?
3. What does the partnership say "creates barriers" to providing meaningful SCHIP care to immigrant families?

Dear Chairman [John] Dingell and Ranking Member [Joe] Barton:

As you work to develop legislation to reauthorize the State Children's Health Insurance Program (SCHIP), we, the below-signed members of the Partnership for Medicaid, a non-partisan, nationwide coalition of safety net providers and other organizations dedicated to improving the Medicaid program, call your attention to several reauthorization issues important to the safety net provider community and critical to ensuring that all of the nation's children have health care coverage.

For nearly ten years, SCHIP has played a major role and has been remarkably successful in providing a safety net to children and adolescents who otherwise might be uninsured. Yet, despite this success, there are still some 9 million children living in the United States who lack coverage for basic health care. This is unacceptable.

SCHIP reauthorization provides Congress an opportunity to strengthen this critically important program, and to expand health insurance coverage to many of the nation's uninsured children. Accordingly, we urge you to consider the following set of recommendations:

Ensuring Financial Support

Ensure Sufficient New Program Funding It is vital that Congress deliver on its pledge to children's health coverage by providing, at a minimum, the full $50 billion in new funds for SCHIP and Medicaid allowed for in the congressional budget resolution. This level of funding is the minimum amount that will suffice to allow states to sustain their existing SCHIP programs, reach a significant share of the uninsured children already eligible for SCHIP and Medicaid, and support ongoing state efforts to expand coverage. It is imperative that states are provided with a predictable and stable source of funding that enables them to continue to move forward in their effort to cover eligible children.

Preserve Coverage for Current Enrollees Since 1997, several states have secured approval through the CMS [Centers for Medicare & Medicaid Services] waiver process to enroll low-income parents in the SCHIP program. In its recent SCHIP Interim Policy Statement, the National Governors Association seeks to maintain state flexibility with the specific objective of continuing this important policy. The Partnership believes that SCHIP reauthorizaton should not increase the number of uninsured Americans, such as by cutting off children in more moderate-income families who cannot afford coverage entirely on their own or by weakening family-based coverage programs operated under SCHIP waivers.

Reaching Children in Need

Strengthen and Improve Program Benefit Package Low-income children are suffering as a result of the myriad of health disparities they face and are more likely to suffer from various illnesses and health conditions. Many of these children are at high risk of developing chronic health conditions. Congress must act to eliminate existing provisions in SCHIP that permit mental health to be offered at 75% of benchmark equivalent plans and that make dental and vision benefits optional. The Partnership supports legislation for SCHIP that requires mental health benefit parity, a dental benefit guarantee and the option for states to provide wrap around dental, vision and mental health benefits for low income children that have health coverage in the private market but are income-eligible for SCHIP.

Promote Streamlined Enrollment and Increased Outreach The Partnership supports allowing states to utilize new tools and procedures to reach the majority of uninsured children currently eligible for, but not enrolled in Medicaid or SCHIP. In particular, the Partnership supports the use of streamlined enrollment processes, such as "Express Lane" enrollment, that allows the use of financial information from other programs (such as school lunch and WIC [Women, Infants, and Children programs]) in determining eligibility. In addition, Congress should make available expanded resources to states for outreach to educate the parents of uninsured children about SCHIP and Medicaid. Furthermore, additional resources ought to be made available (through enhanced federal funding in Medicaid) to states that successfully enroll more eligible children in SCHIP.

Eliminate Negative Impact of Medicaid Documentation Requirements Since enactment in 2006, the Medicaid documentation requirements have had a major and measurable impact on patients and providers, with a number of states reporting significant declines in Medicaid enrollment among children, certain legal immigrants and other clearly eligible citizens. To that end, Congress should ensure that states are allowed as much flexibility as possible to assure that current recipients and new applicants impacted by the law have the broadest opportunity to meet the requirement without losing or being denied Medicaid or SCHIP coverage.

Eliminate Five-Year Prohibition for Lawfully Residing Immigrant Children, and Ensure Access to Viable Language Assistance Services States ought to be given the option to make

Who Receives SCHIP Assistance

The State Children's Health Insurance Program (SCHIP), created under Title XXI of the Social Security Act, expands health coverage to uninsured children whose families earn too much for Medicaid but too little to afford private coverage. It builds on Medicaid, the federal-state health insurance program. . . . Because Medicaid allows states flexibility in determining eligibility, states currently cover children whose family incomes range generally from below the federal poverty level (FPL) to as high as 350 percent FPL. The majority of sates' Medicaid programs cover children in families between 100 and 150 percent of the FPL. . . . In the SCHIP program, states may either cover children in families whose incomes are above the Medicaid eligibility threshold but less than 200 percent of the poverty level, or up to 50 percentage points over the state's current Medicaid income limit for children. Most states provide SCHIP coverage for children in families at or above 200 percent of the poverty level.

USDA Food and Nutrition Service, February 2, 2001.

Medicaid and SCHIP coverage available to lawfully residing immigrant children and pregnant women, as provided for in the Legal Immigrant Children's Health Improvement Act of 2007. In addition, it ought to be noted that the lack of viable language assistance services in Medicaid and SCHIP creates barriers to and diminishes the quality of health care for limited English proficient (LEP) individuals in these programs. In fact, along these lines, most state Medicaid and SCHIP programs do not directly pay for the costs of hiring interpreters or translating essential healthcare information. Therefore,

Congress ought to significantly increase the federal share of the costs of language services so that more states will have the ability to assist in meeting the needs of LEP patients.

Review Policies and Safeguards

Provide Meaningful Review of Program Service and Payment Policies The Partnership supports the establishment of the Medicaid and CHIP [same as SCHIP] Payment and Access Commission (MACPAC) to ensure that the access and payment policies of both programs are reviewed on a consistent basis. Providing these reviews is a step in the right direction to ensure that beneficiaries enrolled in both programs receive the level of services outlined in each program's benefit packages and that adjustments are made to accommodate changes in the health care delivery system and beneficiary demographics.

Invest in Health Care Quality for Children Since no cohesive pediatric health care quality program currently exists in SCHIP or Medicaid, the Partnership supports the creation of a new child health quality initiative. The quality initiative should focus on measures that promote the healthy development of children. It should provide the federal government with the authority and resources necessary to fund the development, testing, and use of pediatric quality measures through a consensus development process involving consumers, payers, and providers. The initiative should also encourage state reporting on child health quality, and promote use of standardized quality measures, such as HEDIS [Health Plan Employer Data and Information Set], that allow for uniformity in data collection and comparisons among states and over time.

Thank you for your consideration. We look forward to working with you on these and other issues vital to the future of the nation's children.

| *"States expanded SCHIP coverage well*
  beyond its original intent."

The State Children's Health Insurance Program Should Not Be Expanded

Tom Price

In the following viewpoint, U.S. Representative Tom Price (a Republican from Georgia) argues that the State Children's Health Insurance Program (SCHIP) needs government funding to serve the millions of low-income children in America. However, he contends that some states have abused the program by granting SCHIP funds to undeserving adults and by affording SCHIP funds to families who live well above the poverty line. Because of these abuses, Price asserts, the states are calling for more and more funds that the U.S. government cannot provide. Price maintains that SCHIP should not be greatly expanded in coming years; instead it should be better regulated to serve only those children who are eligible and in need of its services.

As you read, consider the following questions:

1. According to Price, how many states in 2007 were using SCHIP funds to aid adults who had no children?

Tom Price, "Washington or Patients Can Win on SCHIP—It's up to Us," *The Hill*, July 24, 2007. © 2007 Capitol Hill Publishing Corp., a subsidiary of News Communications Inc. Reproduced by permission.

2. As Price explains, what are the differences in the proposed Senate and House bills regarding SCHIP funding?

3. What does Price say the liberal majority in Congress "fears" when it comes to health insurance plans?

In [late 2007], Congress will vote on reauthorizing the State Children's Health Insurance Program (SCHIP). On the surface, this is an opportunity to reauthorize a program that has successfully provided health insurance for millions of children from low-income families. However, if one digs deeper, one will see that this is truly the opening volley in a renewed debate: Washington-controlled bureaucratic medicine versus patient-centered healthcare.

When SCHIP was created a decade ago, those who could not afford private insurance and were ineligible for Medicaid coverage were left with few options. As part of the Balanced Budget Act of 1997, Congress appropriated $40 billion to help states address these needs. However, despite such a large sum of funds, SCHIP began experiencing trouble in 2002 as certain states' annual spending surpassed their annual federal allotments. It was not until recently however, that the total pool of money began to dry up and states no longer could look to roll over funding to cover the gaps.

No New Entitlement Programs

One of the predominant reasons for these shortfalls is that states expanded SCHIP coverage well beyond its original intent. For example, today 14 states cover adults using SCHIP funding when there are still low-income children within their state without insurance. Six of those states cover adults with no children. Also, some states expanded eligibility to 300 to 350 percent of the federal poverty level.

Fair-minded Americans can agree that our children need and deserve access to quality and affordable health care. That is why few will dispute that we should reauthorize this pro-

States Should Pay for SCHIP Expansion

Since its inception, SCHIP has grown in cost and scope, gradually crowding out part of the private insurance market. Efforts to expand the program would further drive up costs and move it in the direction of an entitlement program with an open-ended commitment from American taxpayers. If state officials wish to expand SCHIP, they ought to do so on their own state's dime rather than asking Congress to collect and redistribute taxes from the rest of the country. Congress must take steps to get its existing healthcare obligations under control rather than make the problem worse through an unwise SCHIP expansion.

Nicola Moore and J.D. Foster,
Heritage Foundation Web Memo # 1540,
July 9, 2007.

gram. However, there is a bidding war that has begun, equating tax money spent with compassion and quality care. The two are rarely connected. Our children's health should not be a vehicle for expanding government and establishing what will amount to a new entitlement program—particularly when it will add billions in runaway spending and likely result in a lower quality of healthcare provided to all.

Both the House and Senate will come up with proposals that will amount to billions of dollars in additional funding for SCHIP. On the high end, the House Democrat proposal would reportedly add an additional $50 billion to $80 billion over the next five years and expand the coverage of SCHIP to families with incomes up to 400 percent of the federal poverty level (FPL). At such a level, children in families with an annual income of up to $82,000 would be eligible for taxpayer-funded coverage—not exactly low-income. This would include 90 percent of children who are already covered under private insurance.

The Senate's proposal looks like it would cost around $35 billion and add nearly a twofold increase on cigarette taxes—a popular target.

More reasonably and responsibly, some House Republicans have recommended an increase of roughly $5 billion over the next five years that would provide eligibility for those up to 200 percent of the FPL. This is the income level SCHIP was originally intended to cover.

Even more positive is a proposal being worked on by other House Republicans that would include fundamental tax reform for the purchase of health insurance that would allow more Americans to be covered, while actually costing the federal government (read: American taxpayer) less.

Consumers Should Be in Charge

In the end, the real question to be addressed is: Who should be making personal healthcare decisions—patients and physicians, or Washington?

Fair-minded Americans do not want Washington making their healthcare decisions. They do not want to build a more complicated bureaucracy with their hard-earned tax money. What they do want is affordable healthcare. They want greater choices, and they want portability. And all this can happen if we embrace fundamental reform and a system that ensures patient ownership of health insurance policies.

The SCHIP reauthorization proposal from the left will produce limited benefit at an enormous cost, and we will be ignoring much larger intentions and consequences. We must challenge this current majority, which is plagued with an aversion and fear of free-market principles—patient-centered principles. Congress should be putting Americans in a position to find affordable coverage with their hard-earned money. We can provide the American people with choices and competition that create greater access and affordability.

Everyone wants to protect and provide for America's children. Nobody has a monopoly on compassion for hardworking American families. But a bad situation does not deserve an even worse solution.

The American people know best, not Washington. Patients and physicians should be making healthcare decisions, not Congress. Let us not embrace a "solution" and leadership that increases government regulation and a Washington-controlled bureaucratic healthcare system.

Let us reauthorize SCHIP with principles that respect patients, families and physicians. That would be a victory for all.

Periodical Bibliography

The following articles have been selected to supplement the diverse views presented in this chapter.

Alyssa Bindman	"Major Improvements Possible If States Make Health a Priority," *Nation's Health*, August 2007.
Matthew DoBias	"Two SCHIPs Set Sail. . ." *Modern Healthcare*, August 6, 2007.
Megan Feller	"Health Care Home Run," *State Legislatures*, June 2006.
John Goodman	"Insurance Folly," *Wall Street Journal*, July 27, 2007.
David Gratzer	"First, Do No Harm," *Forbes*, February 12, 2007.
Peter Harkness	"A Call for Action by States," *CQ Weekly*, January 29, 2007.
Bob Herbert	"Young, Ill and Uninsured," *New York Times*, May 19, 2007.
Paul Krugman	"An Immoral Philosophy," *New York Times*, July 30, 2007.
Anita Manning	"Kids Without Enough Insurance Skip Vaccines," *USA Today*, August 8, 2007.
Nation's Health	"Illinois Provides Universal Health Care Coverage for State's Children," January/February 2006.
National Review	"S-Chipping Away at Free Markets," August 13, 2007.
Wall Street Journal	"The SCHIP Revelation," August 9, 2007.
Alex Wayne and Drew Armstrong	"The SCHIP Challenge: Finding Funding," *CQ Weekly*, August 6, 2007.

For Further Discussion

Chapter 1

1. At a time when most politicians and critics—both conservative and liberal—complain about the high cost of health care, Martin Gaynor and Deepti Gudipati are among the few analysts who assert that health care spending is helping people live longer and better lives. Although Gaynor and Gudipati maintain that too much money is spent on health care as opposed to other pressing social concerns, the pair claims that Americans should be spending a high percentage of their income on health care because Americans value the benefits it brings. Do you think Gaynor and Gudipati are right in arguing that Americans should be content to pay more for a service they greatly value—especially because the return on the investment is better care? Explain why or why not.

2. Universal health care has been an issue in the United States for decades, but there is a great segment of the population that has traditionally been fearful of expanding government to take on more and more welfare entitlements. After reading the viewpoints by Senator Barack Obama and John C. Goodman, explain the pros and cons of adopting a system of universal health care in America. Examine the issue from other perspectives by reading articles in periodicals or on the Internet and then state your opinion on why you believe the country will or will not adopt universal care. In framing your answer, explain whether or not you think that another government entitlement is in the best interest of the nation.

3. Carla Howell takes the unusual position that Americans do not need health insurance. She contends that people would

be better off to save the money they waste on insurance to pay for medical emergencies as they occur. After reviewing the arguments made by Risa Lavizzo-Mourey and others in the chapter, do you think Howell's argument is convincing? Would everyone be better served if they dropped insurance coverage? Why or why not?

Chapter 2

1. Ronald Lagoe, Deborah Aspling and Gert Westert observe that consumer driven health care plans are on the rise and will make consumers more responsible for the spending of health care dollars to bring about a more efficient and less costly health care system. Gail Shearer counters that consumers may not be the most knowledgeable purchasers of health care because few possess the time or experience to find bargains in health care and many would skimp on health care to use their money to buy other needed (or unneeded) commodities. After reading these articles (and the pair on health savings accounts in the following chapter), explain whether you are convinced that giving consumers control over health care spending would lead to a better health care system in America. Be sure to consider the impact on costs and personal health maintenance in your answer.

2. Medicare Advantage plans bring managed care organizations into the government subsidized Medicare system. Mark McClellan maintains that such plans help contain costs and induce more recipients to take better advantage of preventative care. The Medical Rights Center insists that these plans are not cost-effective and suffer from patient complaints concerning quality of care. Whose argument do you find more convincing? Explain why.

3. Advocates of disease management stress that maintaining a relationship with patients in order to assist them in following health regimens helps contain costs and can lead

to improved quality of life. It is another possible means of controlling health care expenditures in the United States. After reviewing the various approaches described in this chapter, which if any do you think the country should employ to bring costs down while ensuring high-performance health care? In your answer, explain why your chosen solution is best and why the alternatives would likely fail to deliver on their promises.

Chapter 3

1. What are the potential advantages of health savings accounts (HSAs) as President Bush defines them? What are the possible drawbacks of these accounts as Families USA describes them? Basing your answer on these two viewpoints and any other article you read on the subject, state whether you believe HSAs could bring more expansive health coverage to the millions of Americans who are struggling to afford insurance and those who lack insurance. Explain how you have arrived at this point of view.

2. Michael F. Cannon insists that tax incentives could help level the playing field for those who want to buy private insurance but find it too expensive. Elise Gould believes that providing tax breaks to private plans will only ruin the risk pool of collective employer-based insurance, leaving the more sickly and needy in employer-based plans that will suffer rising premiums. Do you think private insurance tax breaks are appropriate? Explain why or why not using arguments from the viewpoints.

3. President George W. Bush has tried to arrest ever-increasing health care costs by giving Americans more control over their health care. He has championed health savings accounts as a means of allowing individuals the power to save for future emergencies; he has pushed for tax breaks for people who seek out their own insurance coverage; and he has called for the portability of insur-

ance so that there is no interruption in benefits or care when a worker moves from one job to another. If you had the power to make one of these solutions achieve its optimal effect, which would you choose? Explain why.

Chapter 4

1. Nick Dupree, Michelle Chen, and Stephen A. Moses offer differing opinions on problems with Medicaid and its funding. After reading these viewpoints, describe what changes in the Medicaid system you would make. In framing your answer, specifically address whether you would increase funds for Medicaid, how you would make sure Medicaid funds are delivered to the deserving, and whether you would raise Medicaid co-payments in an effort to defray some of the mounting costs of this program.

2. Both Tom Price and Stephen A. Moses contend that undeserving individuals are abusing state welfare programs such as Medicaid and SCHIP and thus driving up their cost. What policy would you devise to remove undeserving people from these welfare rolls? How would you monitor and enforce your policy (and what would this enforcement cost)? Do you think that eliminating the undeserving will ultimately make these programs more solvent in most states? Why or why not?

Organizations to Contact

The editors have compiled the following list of organizations concerned with the issues debated in this book. The descriptions are derived from materials provided by the organizations. All have publications or information available for interested readers. The list was compiled on the date of publication of the present volume; the information provided here may change. Be aware that many organizations may take several weeks or longer to respond to inquiries, so allow as much time as possible.

American Association of Retired Persons (AARP)
601 E St. NW, Washington, DC   20049
(888) 687-2277
Web site: www.aarp.org

AARP, a membership organization for those over the age of 50, is dedicated to ensuring a high quality of life for individuals as they age. Programs of the organization include public education and community service, advocacy and policy change, and the provision specialized services for members. AARP instituted the Divided We Fail program in an effort to ensure that all Americans have the opportunity to receive quality, affordable health care through programs such as Social Security and Medicare without creating a financial burden on future generations. Additionally, the organization has produced videos such as *In America* as well as press releases and fact sheets chronicling the current state of health care and health insurance in the United States.

American Enterprise Institute (AEI)
1150 Seventeenth St. NW, Washington, DC   20036
(202) 862-5800 • fax: (202) 862-7177
Web site: www.aei.org

AEI is a private, nonpartisan organization providing pertinent information and analysis of current public policy issues in the United States. The institute studies public policy from three primary angles (economics, domestic society and politics, and defense and foreign policy), always promoting the ideals of a free, open market society in which capitalism, democracy, and liberty are cornerstones. AEI has funded the Medicare Reform Series to analyze the impact of federal health care policies on American society; the book *The Diagnosis and Treatment of Medicare* by Andrew J. Rettenmaier and Thomas R. Saving is part of this series. In addition, numerous fact sheets, reviews, and articles on health care topics are available on the organization's Web site.

American Society of Law, Medicine & Ethics (ASLME)
765 Commonwealth Ave., Suite 1634, Boston, MA   02215
(617) 262-4990 • fax: (617) 437-7596
e-mail: info@aslme.org
Web site: www.aslme.org

Beginning with its founding in 1911, ASLME has provided scholars and professionals in fields such as medicine, law, and ethics the opportunity to discuss and analyze important health-related issues. The organization prides itself on incorporating the perspectives of individuals from various backgrounds. *The Journal of Law, Medicine, and Ethics* and *The American Journal of Law & Medicine* are the organization's official periodicals, providing peer-reviewed chronicles of ASLME issues such as public health; race, ethnicity, or economic-based inequality in access to health care; patients' rights with regard to safe and high-quality health care; and the ethical advancement of biomedical science and research.

Brookings Institution
1775 Massachusetts Ave. NW, Washington, DC   20036
(202) 797-6000 • fax: (202) 797-6004
e-mail: webmaster@brookings.edu
Web site: www.brook.edu

The Brookings Institution is a private, public policy research institution seeking to provide accurate and thorough analysis and suggestions to policy makers on the most important issues of the day. The organization studies domestic and global topics from a nonpartisan point of view. The Engelberg Center for Health Care Reform was created by the institution in 2007 in an effort to provide realistic, applicable solutions to health care related problems such as access, quality, and cost. This center's Web site provides the opinions and studies of its scholars on policies that would provide health care for individuals with no health insurance, and other timely issues.

Cato Institute
1000 Massachusetts Ave. NW, Washington, DC   20001-5403
(202) 842-0200 • fax: (202) 842-3490
Web site: www.cato.org

A libertarian organization founded in 1977, the Cato Institute provides public policy research and analysis of contemporary government debates. Cato presents findings through the tri-annual publication, the *Cato Journal*, as well as topical books, pamphlets, and studies on issues within every realm of public policy. In the area of health care reform, the organization favors an approach consisting of deregulation of the health care industry and use of health savings accounts, arguing that this will provide consumers access to their desired form of care at a reasonable price. Detailed commentary and studies are available on the Cato Web site.

Center for Studying Health System Change (HSC)
600 Maryland Ave. SW #550, Washington, DC   20024
(202) 484-5261 • fax: (202) 484-9258
e-mail: hscinfo@hschange.org
Web site: www.hschange.com

HSC employs a combination of national surveys and individual case studies to provide nonbiased research on health care in the United States in order to inform those on all sides of this public policy debate. The goal of the organization is not to take sides favoring one policy over another; instead it seeks to serve as a provider of information for all individuals in an attempt to create health care policies that are beneficial to all Americans. HSC publications are available online and come in the form of issues briefs, community and tracking reports, journal articles, and commentary, among others.

Healthcare Leadership Council (HLC)
1001 Pennsylvania Ave. NW, Suite 550 South
Washington, DC   20004
(202) 452-8700 • fax: (202) 296-9561
Web site: www.hlc.org

HLC promotes a belief that the U.S. health care system is the best in the world, and that this system will improve based on the principles of private, as opposed to government, ownership and regulation. Additionally, the organization places emphasis on the importance of health care management on the local level, within a community. HLC works directly with Congress to apply this vision of health care on a national level. Comprehensive information concerning HLC's stance on issues such as Americans without health insurance, Medicare, and cost of quality health care is available on the organization's Web site.

Heritage Foundation
214 Massachusetts Ave. NE, Washington, DC   20002-4999
(202) 546-4400 • fax: (202) 546-8328
e-mail: info@heritage.org
Web site: www.heritage.org

The Heritage Foundation is a research institute dedicated to promoting public policy consistent with traditional conservative values such as a free market economy, limited government regulation, and strong national defense. The organization actively offers its solutions to the federal government and the public. With regard to health care policy, the foundation remains consistent with its viewpoint, and publications on specific areas such as children's health insurance programs, health care reform, and Medicaid and Medicare can be found on the organization's Web site.

Institute for Health Freedom (IHF)
1875 Eye St. NW, Suite 500, Washington, DC   20006
(202) 429-6610 • fax: (202) 861-1973
e-mail: feedback@forhealthfreedom.org
Web site: www.forhealthfreedom.org

IHF believes that regulations within the health care industry have limited individual Americans' freedom to choose health care providers and plans that are most appropriate for their individual needs. The IHF is dedicated to promoting a health care system and set of policies that increase "health freedom." The organization provides information to both the public and policymakers in an effort to raise awareness about the benefits of personal health care choice, and in turn, to see the passage of policies protecting this choice. *Health Freedom Watch* is the monthly newsletter, sent by email to subscribers, providing detailed information about issues affecting their health care choices.

National Center for Policy Analysis (NCPA)
12770 Coit Rd., Suite 800, Dallas, TX   75251-1339
(972) 386-6272 • fax: (972) 386-0924
Web site: www.ncpa.org

NCPA is an organization that views private solutions to public policy issues as being favorable when compared with government regulation. Based on this belief, the private sector and competition will foster the creation of a better society than government control. Health savings accounts and other consumer-driven solutions are the favored methods of health care reform for the NCPA. The organization has worked with both *20-20* and Florida governor Jeb Bush to promote these ideas. Numerous studies, policy backgrounders, and analyses regarding healthcare policy are available on the NCPA's Web site.

National Coalition on Health Care
1200 G St. NW, Washington, DC   20005
(202) 638-7151

e-mail: info@nchc.org
Web site: www.nchc.org

The National Coalition on Health Care is a nonprofit, nonpartisan organization dedicated to achieving affordable, quality health care for all Americans. Two former presidents, George H. W. Bush and Jimmy Carter, sit as honorary co-chairmen visibly representing the group's nonpartisan nature. The organization has produced the fact sheets *Health Insurance Coverage*, *Health Insurance Cost*, and *Health Insurance Quality*, among others, all of which are available on the coalition's Web site.

Urban Institute (UI)
2100 M St. NW, Washington, DC   20037
(202) 833-7200
Web site: www.urban.org

UI works to evaluate both economic and social policy with regard to urban centers in the United States. The organization publishes its findings to the public and policy makers both domestically and worldwide. Focus areas within the organization's research include crime and justice, housing, education, and health and health care. Reports published by the institute, such as "Why Do People Lack Health Insurance?" and "Issues in Focus: Health Insurance Trends," are available online. Books published by the UI include *Health Policy and the Uninsured* and *Medicare: A Policy Primer*.

Bibliography of Books

Henry J. Aaron and William B. Schwarts, with Melissa Cox — *Can We Say No? The Challenge of Rationing Health Care.* Washington, DC: Brookings Institution, 2005.

Donald L. Bartlett and James B. Steele — *Critical Condition: How Health Care in America Became Big Business—and Bad Medicine.* New York: Doubleday, 2004.

Robert S. Bonney — *Consumer-Directed Healthcare and Its Implications for Providers.* Chicago, IL: Health Administration Press, 2005.

Lawton Robert Burns — *The Business of Healthcare Innovation.* New York: Cambridge University Press, 2005.

Daniel Callahan and Angela A. Wasunna — *Medicine and the Market: Equity v. Choice.* Baltimore, MD: Johns Hopkins University Press, 2006.

Michael F. Cannon — *Healthy Competition: What's Holding Back Health Care and How to Free It.* Washington, DC: Cato Institute, 2005.

John F. Cogan, R. Glenn Hubbard, and Daniel P. Kessler — *Healthy, Wealthy, and Wise: Five Steps to a Better Health Care System.* Washington, DC: AEI, 2005.

Jonathan Cohn — *Sick: The Untold Story of America's Health Care Crisis—and the People Who Pay the Price.* New York: Harper Collins, 2007.

David M. Cutler   *Your Money or Your Life: Strong Medicine for America's Health Care System.* New York: Oxford University Press, 2004.

Jonathan Engel   *Poor People's Medicine: Medicaid and American Charity Care Since 1965.* Durham, NC: Duke University Press, 2006.

Newt Gingrich, Dana Pavey, and Anne Woodbury   *Saving Lives & Saving Money.* Washington, DC: Alexis de Tocqueville Institution, 2003.

David Gratzer   *The Cure: How Capitalism Can Save American Healthcare.* New York: Encounter, 2006.

George C. Halvorson   *Health Care Reform Now! A Prescription for Change.* San Francisco, CA: Jossey-Bass, 2007.

Regina Herzlinger   *Who Killed Health Care? America's $2 Trillion Medical Problem and the Consumer-Driven Cure.* New York: McGraw-Hill, 2007.

David Hyman   *Medicare Meets Mephistopheles.* Washington, DC: Cato Institute, 2006.

Timothy Stoltzfus Jost   *Health Care at Risk: A Critique of the Consumer-Driven Movement.* Durham, NC: Duke University Press, 2007.

Maggie Mahar   *Money-Driven Medicine: The Real Reason Health Care Costs So Much.* New York: Harper Collins, 2006.

Rick Mayes	*Universal Coverage: The Elusive Quest for National Health Insurance.* Ann Arbor, MI: University of Michigan Press, 2004.
Hank McKinnell	*A Call To Action: Taking Back Healthcare for Future Generations.* New York: McGraw Hill, 2005.
David Mechanic	*The Truth About Health Care: Why Reform Is Not Working in America.* Piscataway, NJ: Rutgers University Press, 2006.
David Mechanic, Lynn B. Roqut, and David C. Colby	*Policy Challenges in Modern Health Care.* Piscataway, NJ: Rutgers University Press, 2005.
Sally C. Pipes	*Miracle Cure: How to Solve America's Health Care Crisis and Why Canada Isn't the Answer.* San Francisco, CA: Pacific Research Institute, 2004.
Michael E. Porter and Elizabeth Olmsted Teisberg	*Redefining Health Care: Creating Value-Based Competition on Results.* Boston: Harvard Business School Publishing, 2006.
Jill Quadagno	*One Nation Uninsured: Why the U.S. Has No National Health Insurance.* New York: Oxford University Press, 2005.
Dr. Arnold Relman	*A Second Opinion: Rescuing America's Health Care.* New York: Public Affairs, 2007.

Susan Sered and Rushika Fernandopulle

Uninsured in America: Life and Death in the Land of Opportunity. Berkeley, CA: University of California Press, 2005.

David A. Shore, ed.

The Trust Crisis in Healthcare: Causes, Consequences, and Cures. New York: Oxford University Press, 2007.

Don M. Sloan and Robin Feman

Practicing Medicine Without a License: The Corporate Takeover of Healthcare in America. Ashland, OR: Caveat, 2006.

Rosemary A. Stevens, Charles E. Rosenberg, and Lawton R. Burns, eds.

History and Health Policy in the United States: Putting the Past Back In. Piscataway, NJ: Rutgers University Press, 2006.

Index